CONTENTS

Preface   v

Introduction   New Product and Brand Management Software (Version 1.0)   1

Chapter 1   Tutorial for Cluster Analysis   15
                       Conglomerate Inc's New PDA Case   27

Chapter 2   Tutorial for the GE Portfolio Planning Model (GE)   31
                       Product Planning at Addison Wesley Longman Case   38

Chapter 3   Tutorial for Positioning Analysis   47
                       Positioning the Infiniti G20 Case   55
                       Positioning the ConneCtor Exercise   62

Chapter 4   Tutorial for Conjoint Analysis   65
                       Forte Hotel Design Case   83

Chapter 5   Tutorial for the Assessor Pretest Market Model (ASSESSOR)   91
                       Johnson Wax: Enhance (A) Case   102

Chapter 6   Tutorial for the Generalized Bass Model (GBass)   133
                       Zenith High Definition Television (HDTV) Case   143

INDEX   151

To my love and best friend,
Dorothy, for sharing her time
with one more book.

-Gary

To Ann for her love and support,
and Cara for providing the
needed distraction.

-Arvind

PREFACE

Rapid changes in the marketplace, in data, and in the computing environment are transforming the structure and content of the marketing manager's job. As a profession, marketing is evolving so that it is no longer based primarily on conceptual content. While many view traditional marketing as an art and some view it as a science, the new marketing increasingly looks like engineering (that is, combining art and science to solve specific problems).

There will always be a role for marketing concepts. Indeed, to make use of the powerful information tools now available requires sound conceptual grounding. But marketers need more than concepts to fully exploit the resources available to them. They need to move beyond conceptual marketing toward what we call marketing engineering: the use of interactive computer decision models to help support marketing decisions.

This package of materials is designed to supplement a course in New Product or Brand Management. It includes selections from our book, *Marketing Engineering* (Addison Wesley Longman, 1998) that are appropriate for such courses. Those selections are designed to make the corresponding course material come alive with hands-on exercises and cases.

Although each piece of software included here has associated with it a corresponding case or problem, all of the software (except the AS-SESSOR spreadsheet) is independent of those cases and can be used separately on other case-problems or on real problems.

According to most new product and brand management texts, the most common analytic problems correspond to segmentation, targeting and positioning, product design and new product forecasting. We have selected the material in this book to meet those needs.

1. **Needs-based Segmentation Using Cluster Analysis**: This general software tool performs cluster analysis, factor analysis and discriminant analysis. The accompanying case addresses how to segment the market on the basis of needs for a sample of prospective buyers for a new personal digital assistant. The case raises issues such as: (1) How many segments should the firm consider (and how do those segments differ)? (2) Which of those segments should the firm target? (see GE model below). (3) How many different products should the firms offer? (also linked to GE model). (4) How should the new product be positioned? (see Positioning Analysis, below).

2. **Targeting/Business Prioritization Using GE/McKinsey Approach**: This software tool allows the user to build a customized portfolio of SBUs (Strategic Business Units) and associated attribute dimensions and weights to help prioritize the businesses. The ac-

companying case looks at a portfolio of four existing SBUs at Conglomerate Inc. (but the tool may be used more generally and can be applied to the PDA case as well).

3. **Product Positioning Using Perceptual Mapping**: This software tool takes customer perceptions and preferences for products and produces a two- or three-dimensional map that allows the user to view alternative product positions and consider the strategic implications of changes in that positioning. The accompanying case looks at positioning the Infiniti G20 in 1990: given customer perceptions and preferences for new cars in 1990, how should Infiniti position this car in the market. (We also include a data set and exercise that is related to the PDA segmentation case).

4. **Product Design Using Conjoint Analysis**: This software implements the full-profile version of conjoint analysis. The program allows users to (1) construct the conjoint design by specifying new product attributes and options, (2) obtain data from customers for the chosen design, and (3) conduct market simulations using data from customers to determine the product design(s) that will generate the highest market share(s). We include a hotel design exercise for Forte Hotels to illustrate the use of conjoint analysis.

5. **New Product Assessment and Forecasting using the ASSESSOR Model**: The ASSESSOR system is a set of measurement procedures and models designed to help managers assess the market share for new packaged goods before test marketing. Our implementation includes two of the system's core models: the trial and Repeat model and the Preference model. This implementation has been customized to accompany the Harvard Business School Case: Johnson Wax: Enhance (A), reprinted here.

6. **New Product Forecasting Using the Generalized Bass Model**: The Bass model captures many of the market dynamics associated with the introduction, adoption and early sales trajectory of new products (durable goods in particular) and new technologies. Our implementation includes the original version of the model as well as the generalized Bass model, which includes the effect of advertising and price changes on the sales trajectory of the new product. The model can be calibrated from our library of analogous products or from early sales data. We include an abridged version of the Harvard Business school case, Zenith High Definition television (HDTV) where the model can be applied.

The pedagogic philosophy here involves two main principles: learning by doing and end-user modeling. What this means is that the way you will learn these concepts best is to try to apply the software to the problem and make some specific recommendations based on your analyses. Thus you learn the concept by doing it yourself—not merely by studying the concept or by assigning the analysis to some staff member or consultant.

This volume contains both software tutorials (step by step instructions on how to use the software) as well as the problem sets or cases that are keyed to the concept. *We strongly recommend that you go through each tutorial (making sure you can reproduce the results there) before attempting to "solve" the case.* Our experience is that well over 90% of the difficulties users have running the software are solved by simply reproducing the screens in the respective tutorial.

Also, read the first section of this tutorial carefully—it not only tells you how to install the software, but it provides a number of other general hints about using the software.

To get other software hints and updates, please visit our website: *http://hepg.awl.com/lilien-rangaswamy/mktgeng/*. You can also send us your comments and suggestions about the software by using the e-mail facility available at this site.

Acknowledgments

This book grew out of the multi-year effort that we have termed *Marketing Engineering* and represents an evolution of our vision to put marketing modeling concepts and tools into more general use. We gratefully acknowledge the support of the companies that sponsor Penn State's Institute for the Study of Business Markets, whose generous support made this entire effort possible. We also thank Mike Roche at Addison Wesley Longman and series editor Joel Steckel at New York University who helped us shape the final product.

While we wrote portions of the software, we were involved more in the design and testing of the actual implementation of the codes. Key software were implemented by Louis Jia, Animesh Karna, Jean-François Latour, John Lin, and Andrew "Nuke" Stollak. Our students, Lakshmi Anand, Tolga Gurkin, Katrin Starke, Selva Vaidiyanathan, and David Wu provided additional, essential support.

The entire manuscript was produced by Mary Wyckoff. In addition to her manuscript preparation, Mary managed the entire process and kept us relaxed and cheerfully on schedule. We are deeply grateful for her dedication to this effort!

We also thank the many early adopters of *Marketing Engineering* whose unwavering support and gentle prods to correct software glitches have helped us to continuously improve this product. Thanks to all!

Gary L. Lilien
Arvind Rangaswamy
June 1998

INTRODUCTION

NEW PRODUCT AND BRAND MANAGEMENT SOFTWARE (VERSION 1.0)

Installing New Product and Brand Management: Marketing Engineering Applications

Installing the software onto your computer's hard disk is an easy process, but you should still read through the entire installation instructions before you start.

A. This software is supplied to you on a CD-ROM. Before you start, make sure that you have the proper hardware and operating system:

   Minimum configuration: IBM-compatible PCs running the 486 processor (33 MHz), 16 MB RAM, 15 MB available hard disk space, and a CD-ROM drive.

   Recommended configuration: IBM-compatible PCs running the Pentium or equivalent processor (133 MHz or better), 32MB RAM, 15 MB available hard disk space, and a CD-ROM drive.

   Operating system: Windows 95 and Windows NT.

   Microsoft Excel: Parts of this software require the availability of Microsoft Excel 7 or higher. If you have not installed Excel on your system, you may still be able to use the non-Excel models included in this package.

B. **Installing the software**

   1. Start Windows.

   2. Insert the Marketing Engineering CD-ROM into your CD-ROM drive.

   3. Run the setup.exe application in drive x:\, where x is the letter of your CD-ROM drive.

   4. Follow the instructions on the screen to complete the installation. We recommend that you install this program in the default directory C:\Program Files\MktgEng, although it will work on any non-network (local) drive.

C. ***Uninstalling the software***

1.   Start Windows.

2.   Open **Control Panel**.

3.   Open **Add/Remove Programs**.

4.   Select "Marketing Engineering." Click **Add/Remove** button.

Required add-ins for running Excel applications

For most Excel applications, you need the Solver tool. Solver is not part of the default configuration when you install Microsoft Excel. Under the **Tools** menu on your version of Excel, check the list of **Add-Ins** to see whether they are included. If not, run the Excel (or MS Office) setup procedure (with the original installation disks or CD) and select the appropriate options to install Solver.

Setting up Marketing Engineering after installation

Setting preferences: If you wish to customize the location of the files used by the program, go to the **Help** menu and select **Preferences**. In particular, make sure that the path to Excel.exe is correctly specified.

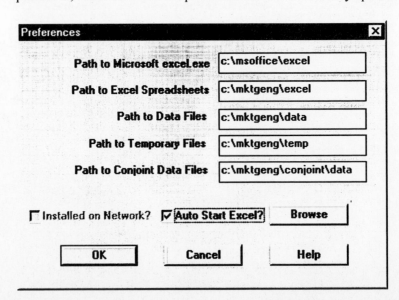

You can install the software on a network only with the network version of Marketing Engineering. If you check **Auto Start Excel,** the program will automatically start Excel every time you open Marketing Engineering. If you turn off this option, you can still open Excel whenever you want to by going to the **File** menu and choosing **Open Excel**.

Opening applications: When you start Marketing Engineering, you will briefly see the following screen:

On the **Model** menu select a model, e.g., **Positioning Analysis**.

NOTE: *Only models that appear as active menu items can be opened. The non-activated items are part of the full Marketing Engineering suite of programs.*

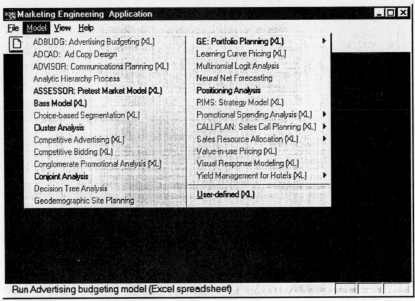

Tips for using the software

Marketing Engineering consists of three different types of software modules:

1. Windows-based programs that will run directly off the Marketing Engineering main menu:
    -   Cluster Analysis
    -   Positioning Analysis

2. Spreadsheet models that will be loaded under Excel:
    -   Generalized Bass Model
    -   ASSESSOR Pretest Market Model
    -   GE: Portfolio Planning

3. A stand-alone application that is "loosely" connected to the main menu and is simply executed when invoked:
    -   Conjoint Analysis

Select **Index** under the **Help** menu to get information about individual models and how to run them.

NOTE: *The following tips apply only to software modules that are **Microsoft Excel applications**.*

Opening Excel models directly: You can open Excel models directly by clicking on *.xls files located in the (default) directory, C:\Program Files\MktgEng\Excel. This can be helpful if you have limited memory on your computer system to load the full Marketing Engineering program. If you move the Excel files to a new directory, make sure that the file modgen97.ind is also located in the new directory.

Moving between the main Marketing Engineering window and an Excel application: To move back and forth between the Marketing Engineering main window and an Excel application you can use the ALT+TAB key combination. You can also get back to the Marketing Engineering main window from an Excel application by going to the **Model** menu and clicking **Back to Mktg. Eng.**

Entering data into a Excel spreadsheet: After you enter data in a cell, press the Enter key to ensure that the data gets registered within the spreadsheet.

Using Solver: In some cases the Solver runs in Excel will not converge. You may then have to provide Solver with new starting values. See Appendix at the end of the section of tips for using Solver.

Unprotecting locked cells: If you want to make changes to locked cells or if you want to unprotect the spreadsheet for certain Solver runs, go to the **Tools** menu, select **Protection**, and click **Unprotect**.

Saving Excel files: If you want to save any of the Excel spreadsheets that you modify, save it in the same directory (default: C:\Program Files\MktgEng\Excel) in which the other Excel files are located.

Non US Versions of Excel: Much of our code assumes that you will be using English/American conventions for numbers and currency. The most critical problem is the difference between the use of the "." and the "," to refer to decimals depending on the country you are in. You must use US conventions in your input and you must make the following system modifications to run the programs with a non-US version of Excel.

First, Close any open programs.

Next, Click the **Start Button**, point to **Settings**, click **Control Panel**.

Next, Double Click Regional Settings.

Select English (United States) as indicated below and first click **Apply** and then **OK**:

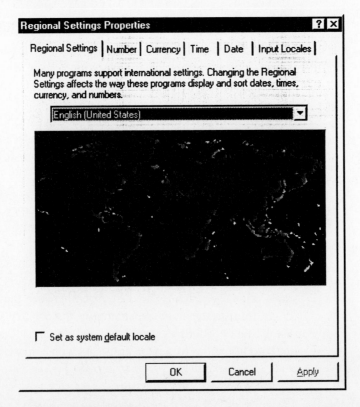

(You may be requested to insert the Windows CD at this time.)

Select the Number and Currency tabs and check to see that the US conventions are now applied.

Regional Settings Properties

Regional Settings | **Number** | Currency | Time | Date | Input Locales

Appearance samples

Positive: 123,456,789.00   Negative: -123,456,789.00

Decimal symbol: .

No. of digits after decimal: 2

Digit grouping symbol: ,

No. of digits in group: 3

Negative sign symbol: -

Negative number format: -1.1

Display leading zeros: 0.7

Measurement system: U.S.

List separator: ,

OK   Cancel   Apply

Regional Settings Properties

Regional Settings | Number | **Currency** | Time | Date | Input Locales

Appearance samples

Positive: $123,456,789.00   Negative: ($123,456,789.00)

¤ = Universal currency symbol

Currency symbol: $

Positive currency format: ¤1.1

Negative currency format: (¤1.1)

Decimal symbol: .

No. of digits after decimal: 2

Digit grouping symbol: ,

No. of digits in group: 3

OK   Cancel   Apply

After you have completed these changes, Click the **Start Button** again, then click **Shut Down** and Click **Restart the Computer** and finally Click **OK**.

This procedure will allow you to run our software.

Be sure to reset to your local conventions when you are done using our software!

NOTE: *The following tips apply only to software modules that run directly off the main menu, namely, Cluster Analysis and Positioning Analysis.*

Incorporating your own data sets: There are three ways to create new data sets for Cluster Analysis and Positioning Analysis.

1. **Load an ASCII file containing the data in the appropriate format**: Use a standard word processing program to generate a text file that can be directly read by the program. The format for the file follows:

Perceptual Mapping	Line 1
3 4	Line 2
5.6 6.0 4.6 3.6	Section 1
4.4 3.6 5.2 2.2	
2.9 6.4 2.7 2.6	
Sprint	Section 2
MCI	
AT&T	
Other	
Value	Section 3
Service	
Special Programs	

   Line 1: Enter title of data set
   Line 2: Enter the number of rows and the number of columns of data
   Section 1: Enter the data (separate by comma or space)
   Section 2: Enter column headings
   Section 3: Enter row headings

   You can load this file into Marketing Engineering by selecting **File**, followed by **Open**. You will be prompted for the file name.

2. **Import data from Excel**: First, open the Marketing Engineering program. From the **File** menu, select **New**.

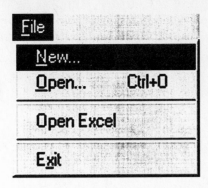

Enter a file name and click **OK** to see the following screen.

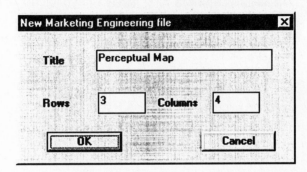

Enter a title for the data and the number of rows and columns. Click **OK.**

Next, separately enter or import a data set into Excel (just the data, no labels) as shown below:

You can now import the data from Excel into Marketing Engineering in one of the following two ways:

Copy and paste the data directly into Marketing Engineering. In Excel, select the data range you want to import into Marketing Engineering. From the **Edit** menu use **Copy** or **Cut** to paste the data to Windows clipboard. Use the ALT+TAB key combination to get to the Marketing Engineering window. Place the cursor on the first row and first column of the blank spreadsheet and paste the data from Excel onto the Marketing Engineering worksheet. If you want to override the default column and row headings, enter the new names by selecting Marketing Engineering's **Edit** menu and then **Edit Row Labels** or **Edit Column Labels**.

Import as an Excel 4.0 file: Save the data as an Excel 4.0 worksheet. Go to the **File** menu in Marketing Engineering and select **Import Excel**. You will be prompted for the file name.

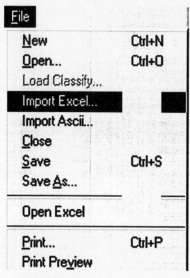

3. *Import just data from an ASCII file*: First open the Marketing Engineering program. From the **File** menu, select **New**. You will be prompted to provide a title for the data and the number of rows and columns.

Now load a text file that contains just the data (the 3 × 4 data set above), one record per line with data separated by a space or tab. Position the cursor on the first row and first column of the spreadsheet. On the **File** menu, select **Import ASCII**. You will prompted for the file name.

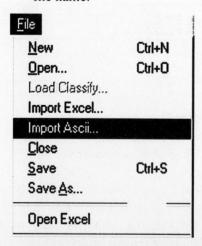

If you wish to override the default column and row headings, enter the new names directly on the spreadsheet by going to the **Edit** menu and selecting **Edit Row Labels** or **Edit Column Labels**.

4. ***Enter the data manually***: On the **File** menu click **New**. You will be prompted to provide a title for the data and the number of rows and columns. Next you can enter data in the blank spreadsheet starting with the first column of the first row.

Viewing the data: Once you have entered or imported data into Marketing Engineering, you will see a graphical display of the data.

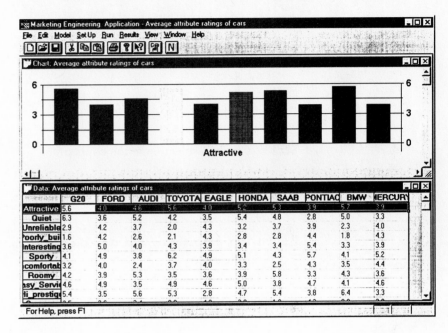

By clicking on a column or row header on the spreadsheet you can obtain a graphical display of the data in that column or row. You can also simultaneously display any subset of the data by dragging the mouse over the desired cells. On the **Edit** menu, you can use **Insert** and **Delete** to make changes to the data.

Changing row and column labels: On the **Edit** menu use **Edit Row Labels** and **Edit Column Labels** to make changes.

Modifying data: You can make changes to the data directly on the spreadsheet. These changes will be incorporated the next time you run the model. However the changes will not be saved for the future unless you specifically save them by going to the **File** menu and choosing **Save** or **Save As**.

Description of the Icons on Marketing Engineering toolbar. On the main window of Marketing Engineering, you will see the following toolbar:

Below is a short description of the each of the items on the toolbar:

Tool	Description
	Creates a new marketing engineering data worksheet.
	Opens an existing marketing engineering data worksheet.
	Saves the currently loaded file.
	Cuts a selection and places it on the Windows clipboard.
	Copies a selection to the clipboard.
	Pastes the contents of the clipboard.
	Prints the active data worksheet according to the current print settings.
	Displays marketing engineering version and copyright information.
	Opens the main help file for marketing engineering.
	Runs the selected program (Cluster Analysis or Positioning Analysis).
	Displays next chart in Positioning Analysis.

APPENDIX
Tips for Using Solver

The Solver implemented in Excel (produced by a software firm called Frontline Systems) uses numerical methods to solve equations and to optimize linear and nonlinear functions with either continuous variables (as in advertising spending) or integer variables (number of account-visits in a quarter). The methods used are iterative; generally Solver calculates how small changes in the decision variables affect the value of the objective function. If the objective function improves (e.g., if profit increases), Solver moves the decision variables in that direction. If the objective function gets worse, Solver moves in the opposite direction. If the objective function cannot be improved by either an increase or a decrease in any of the decision variables, Solver stops, reporting at least a local solution. In using Solver, you should be aware of the following situations that might occur:

1. ***Local optima***: While Solver may have found the top of a hill (the highest point in the region), there may be a higher peak elsewhere. Solver would have to go DOWN from the local peak and begin searching elsewhere to find it. In other words, Solver would need a new starting value ("By Changing Variable" cells in the "Solver Parameter" box) to find the optimum.

   Example: The following is an S-shaped advertising spending function to be optimized. Suppose that we started Solver with the level of advertising = 0. Note that advertising spending cannot be negative and that profit initially decreases with increases in advertising spending because we have an advertising response model with a threshold. Hence Solver cannot decrease advertising spending to less than zero (because of the constraint) and it does not want to go up (as, locally, at least, that would decrease profitability), and so we are at a local maximum. However, if we start the problem with advertising at 1.0 or greater, Solver will correctly find the optimum value at $7.25.

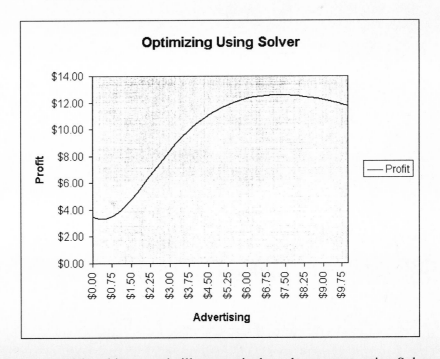

What this example illustrates is that when you are using Solver, you may need to try different starting values to be sure that you have reached a global optimal solution. Some of our Excel spreadsheets have built-in options that permit you to try a different starting value if Solver fails to converge or gives you a local solution.

2. **No feasible solution**: Suppose that we set two constraints: $X > 6$ and $X < 3$. Clearly both of these constraints cannot be satisfied at the same time, and Solver will fail to provide any solution. While the example here makes the lack of any fea sible solution obvious, in larger problems this is often quite subtle.

3. **Other problems**: General nonlinear optimizers like Excel's Solver are remarkable technical additions to the analyst's toolkit. With their power and flexibility come a variety of other problems, however. The user who wants to use Solver directly in market analyses or who wants to adapt or adjust the operation of some of the software that uses Solver may run into a number of other questions or problems, many of which are addressed in Excel's User's Guide.

   Some of those problems are caused by the way the user formulates the specific problem and employs Solver's options. Other problems may be caused by bugs in your version as of Excel and in Excel's link to your operating system (your version of Windows). If the results you are getting do not make sense, it may help to quit Windows or even to reboot your computer before trying to solve the problem again.

Chapter 1

TUTORIAL FOR CLUSTER ANALYSIS

Concept

Markets are heterogeneous. Customers differ in their values, needs, wants, constraints, beliefs, and incentives to act in a particular way. Products compete with one another in attempting to satisfy the needs and wants of those customers. By segmenting the market, firms can better understand their customers and target their marketing efforts efficiently and effectively. Through segmentation, an organization strives to attain a happy middle ground where it does not rely on a common marketing program for all customers, nor does it incur the high costs of developing a unique program for each customer.

Three definitions are critical to the concept of segmentation:

A *market segment* is a group of actual or potential customers who can be expected to respond in a similar way to a product or service offer. That is, they want the same types of benefits or solutions to problems from the product or service, or they respond in a similar way to a company's marketing communications.

Market segmentation is the process of dividing customers whose valuations of a product or service vary greatly into groups or segments containing customers whose valuations vary very little within the group but vary greatly among groups.

A *target market* is a market that a company chooses to serve effectively and profitably.

There is no single segmentation approach. The marketing problem, the timing, the availability of relevant data, and similar considerations should dictate the appropriate approach.

If the firm has data on customer characteristics (e.g., needs) from a sample of customers, then it can use Cluster Analysis to identify the appropriate segments. Cluster analysis is a set of techniques for discovering structure (groupings) within a complex body of data, such as the data used in segmentation analysis. We can explain the concept by considering a deck of cards. Each card varies from the other cards along three dimensions (variables): suit, color, and number. If you are asked to partition a pack of cards into two distinct groups, you might sort them into red and black, or into numbered cards and picture cards. While you can partition a pack of cards intuitively, partitioning a large number of items into groups can be very complex, especially if those items vary along a number of different dimensions. To form segments in such cases, we have to use formal methods. There are two basic classes of methods:

- Hierarchical methods, in which you build up or break down the data customer by customer (row by row)
- Partitioning methods, in which you break the data into a pre-specified number of segments and then reallocate or swap customers to improve some measure of effectiveness

Our software includes one method of each type—Ward's (1963) (hierarchical) and *K*-means (partitioning).

Hierarchical methods produce "trees" formally called dendograms. Hierarchical methods themselves fall into two categories: build-up (agglomerative) methods and split-down (divisive) methods.

Agglomerative methods generally follow this procedure:

1. At the beginning you consider each item (customer) to be its own cluster.

2. You join the two items that are closest on some chosen measure of distance.

3. You then join the next two closest objects (individual items or clusters), either joining two items to form a group or attaching an item to the existing cluster.

4. Return to step 3 until all items are clustered.

Agglomerative methods differ in how they join clusters to one another. In Ward's method, one of the two methods included in the software, you form clusters based on the change in the error sum of squares associated with joining any pair of clusters.

The most commonly used partitioning method is K-means clustering. The procedure works as follows:

1. Begin with two cluster centers (starting points) and allocate every item (customer) to its nearest cluster center.

2. Reallocate items one at a time to reduce the sum of internal cluster variability until you have minimized the criterion (the sum of the within-cluster-sums of squares) for two clusters.

3. Repeat steps 1 and 2 for three, four, or more clusters.

4. After completing step 3, return to step 1 and repeat the procedure with different starting points until the process converges – you no longer see decreases in the within-cluster sum of squares.

While there are many ways to determine starting points, we recommend using the output of Ward's procedure to give good starting points (this is the procedure used in our software).

In addition to Cluster Analysis, our software includes two associated procedures: (1) Factor Analysis and (2) Discriminant Analysis. In Factor Analysis we reduce a large data set into a smaller data set. Specifically, we analyze the interrelationships among a large number of variables and then represent them in terms of common, underlying factors. Such data reduction is sometimes required in segmentation studies because we have data on a wide battery of attitude and needs variables from a sample of customers. If many of those variables measure similar or interrelated constructs, then the subsequent segmentation analysis could lead to misleading conclusions because some variables are overweighted and others underweighted. In Discriminant Analysis, we identify observable characteristics of customers (e.g., sex, area of residence, media habits, etc.) that maximally discriminate between customers in different segments. By identifying such variables, we will be better able to develop marketing programs to targeted segments.

Software

To run Cluster Analysis, you must have a data file structured so that the rows are customers and the columns are the variables that reflect the preferences or needs of those customers (the segmentation basis variables. If you select the discriminant analysis option, you must identify a second separate data file with the same number of rows (referring to the customers) but possibly with a different number of columns (which reflect the segment descriptors). The needs data and the descriptor data are kept in two separate files to ensure that segmentation criteria and targeting criteria need not, and often will not, be the same.

We illustrate the use of the program below, referring to the exercise on Conglomerate's new PDA. The exercise concerns identifying need-based segments for a new type of Personal Digital Assistant (PDA) and finding a way to target the selected segments. The data for this exercise are in two files:

- PDA.DAT contains information on the needs of sampled customers.
- PDA_DIS.DAT contains information on demographics and other variables relevant to developing a program for targeting a PDA to these customers.

From the **Model** menu, select **Cluster Analysis**. You will be prompted to choose the file containing input data. Use the file PDA.DAT for the exercise. This will load the data into the program.

NOTE: *If you make changes to the data to evaluate alternative solutions, the program will not automatically save these changes. Save the changes (under a separate file name if necessary) by going to the* ***File*** *menu and clicking* ***Save As****.*

Go to the **Set Up** menu to select the parameters for your analysis as shown in the following example:

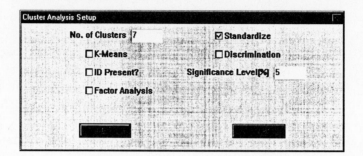

In the area for **No. of Clusters,** you can choose between two and nine clusters (segments) for analysis. If you choose **Standardize**, all variables will be standardized to 0 mean and unit variance before analysis. Choosing this option is a good idea if the variables are measured on different scales, as is the price variable in this example. **Discrimination** allows you to maximally discriminate among the resulting segments using the demographic variables available in PDA_DIS.DAT (the program will prompt you to indicate this file name when needed). **ID Present** allows you to label a case in the data. Such identification is useful in developing segment-specific marketing programs.

NOTE: *The* ***ID Present*** *option is disabled in this educational version of the software.*

As a default, this program uses the Ward's minimum-variance hierarchical-clustering analysis. By selecting **K-Means,** you can run a K-Means clustering algorithm. In this case, the output of hierarchical clustering provides the initial configuration for the K-Means clustering. After you select the options for the run, click **OK**.

If you check **Factor Analysis,** the program will preprocess your input data to identify a set of factors, which it then uses in the cluster analysis procedure. Factor analysis will standardize the variables before finding the underlying factors. However the resulting factor scores, which are then used for cluster analysis, are not standardized. We recommend that you use unstandardized factor scores in the cluster analysis procedure. Thus, you should not check **Standardize** in the setup box.

Next go to the **Run** menu and select **Run Model**. If you selected **Factor Analysis,** you will see the following dialog box that asks you to

procedure (this allows you to override the number of factors recommended by the program).

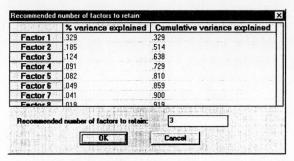

After the program runs, you will see the results of the analysis displayed in the top window. To see the output more clearly, you can maximize this window. In this example, the resulting screen displays the members of the five segments.

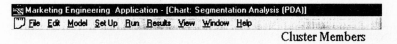

Cluster Members

1	1 4 11 13 28 37 38 42 44 54 62 70 71
2	2 3 5 12 15 18 21 25 27 31 45 48 50 58 59 60 66 67 69 72
3	6 8 16 24 36 39 43 47 49 52 53 55 56 57 61 63 65
4	7 14 20 26 34 35 51 64
5	9 10 17 19 22 23 29 30 32 33 40 41 46 68

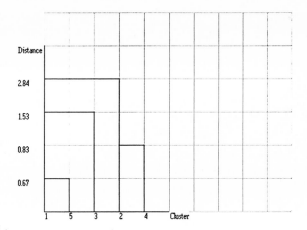

If you scroll down the window, you will see a dendogram showing the distances between the clusters. If you want to remove the grids from the dendogram, go to the **View** menu, choose **View Options**, and clear the check box for **Grid**. (The dendogram is displayed only if you did not choose the K-Means clustering option.)

In this example, clusters 1 and 5 are the closest clusters, separated by a distance of 0.67 units; clusters 2 and 4 are separated by 0.83 units;

and clusters 1 and 3 are separated by 1.53 units. If you decide on a four-cluster solution, the two nearest clusters (1 and 5) will be merged into one cluster. Use the dendogram to select an appropriate number of clusters. (One way to determine the number of clusters is to look for a solution in which the clusters are separated evenly). You can combine clusters that are close to each other by specifying a solution that contains fewer clusters.

You can add descriptive labels to the dendogram. Click anywhere on the screen, and a label dialog box will appear. What you enter in this dialog box will be inserted at the selected location. To delete the labels you entered, go to the **Edit** menu and choose **Delete Labels**.

Marketing Engineering Application - [Chart: Segmentation Analysis (PDA)]

File Edit Model Set Up Run Results View Window Help

Correlation of variables with each significant discriminant function (significance level < .05).

Variable	Func1	Func2	Func3
PDA	.696	.154	.136
Professnl	.682	.063	.264
Income	.660	.099	.203
Bus_Week	.600	-.040	-.023
Education	.553	.021	-.142
M_Gourmet	.464	.069	.184
PC_Mag	.294	.002	.114
Construct	-.300	.670	-.177
Field&Stre	-.245	.552	.110
Emergency	-.184	.481	.038
Age	-.043	-.061	.057
Service	-.334	-.401	.718
Sales	-.106	-.439	-.638
%_Variance			
Explained	41.4	35.1	17.5

For Help, press F1

EXHIBIT 1

Exhibit 1 shows the correlation between each variable and the statistically significant discriminant functions. (This is displayed only if you selected **Discrimination** in the **Set Up** box.) The *absolute magnitude* of this correlation indicates the extent to which a variable discriminates between the clusters. The correlations are ordered from the largest to the smallest in absolute magnitude within each discriminant function. In this example, whether someone is a professional is an important descriptor of the cluster to which that person belongs. The "Professional" variable correlates highly with a discriminant function (Function 1) that explains 41.4 percent of the variation among the respondents included in the study.

To print a copy of the summary results to an attached printer, go to **File** and choose **Print**. To cut and paste these results as an object in another Windows application (e.g., Word for Windows), bring the display window to the foreground, go to the **Edit** menu and select **Cut** or **Copy** and then paste into another Windows application.

You can view an extensive set of associated diagnostics (means of variables in each segment, hit rate, etc.) by going to the **Results** menu and selecting **View Diagnostics**.

If you selected **Factor Analysis,** the first set of diagnostics that you would see is the following table showing variance explained by each factor, the factor score matrix, and the factor-loading matrix.

Diagnostics for factor analysis

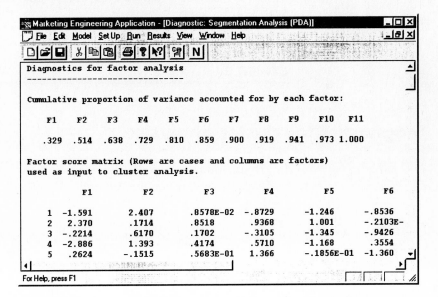

EXHIBIT 2

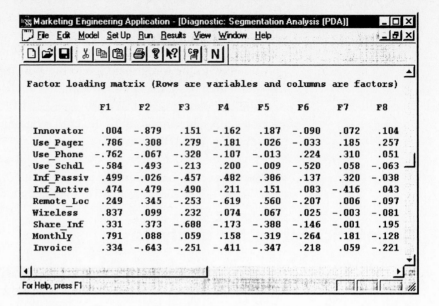

EXHIBIT 3

Diagnostics for cluster analysis

If you did not select **K-Means** in the **Set Up** box, you will see the table shown below for the hierarchical-clustering procedure (Ward's method).

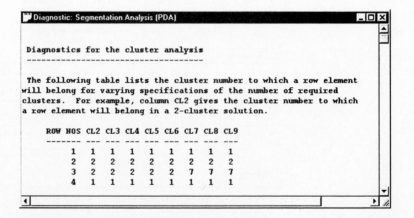

EXHIBIT 4

Exhibit 4 lists the cluster to which a row element (customer) will belong for varying specifications of the number of clusters. For example, row 3 will belong to cluster 2 as long as you specify fewer than seven clusters. If you specify more than seven clusters, this customer will be assigned to cluster 7.

If you selected **K-Means** in the **Set Up** box, you will see the table shown in exhibit 5, giving the probabilities of each row element belonging to each cluster. The probabilities are in inverse proportion to the distance between a customer's characteristics and cluster centroids.

```
Marketing Engineering  Application - [Diagnostic: Segmentation Analysis (PDA)]
 File  Edit  Model  Set Up  Run  Results  View  Window  Help

The following table lists the probabilities of each row element
belonging to each of the clusters for the 5-cluster solution
you specified.  The probabilities are based on the inverse of the
distance between an element and each cluster.


   ROW   CL1    CL2    CL3    CL4    CL5
   ---  -----  -----  -----  -----  -----
    1   .665   .076   .067   .053   .138
    2   .070   .624   .076   .137   .094
    3   .328   .181   .146   .120   .225
    4   .547   .083   .109   .053   .209
    5   .155   .244   .155   .129   .317
    6   .090   .103   .574   .063   .169
    7   .056   .162   .068   .643   .070

For Help, press F1
```

EXHIBIT 5

```
Marketing Engineering  Application - [Diagnostic: Segmentation Analysis (PDA)]
 File  Edit  Model  Set Up  Run  Results  View  Window  Help
```

Actual Cluster	# of cases	Predicted cluster				
		CL1	CL2	CL3	CL4	CL5
CL1	13	6	1	1	2	3
		46.2%	7.7%	7.7%	15.4%	23.1%
CL2	20	2	11	0	2	5
		10.0%	55.0%	.0%	10.0%	25.0%
CL3	17	2	0	13	1	1
		11.8%	.0%	76.5%	5.9%	5.9%
CL4	8	0	0	0	8	0
		.0%	.0%	.0%	100.0%	.0%
CL5	14	4	3	0	1	6
		28.6%	21.4%	.0%	7.1%	42.9%

```
Hit rate: Percent of total cases correctly classified: 61.11

For Help, press F1
```

EXHIBIT 6

Exhibit 6 presents a summary of the predictive validity of the discriminant analysis. The overall hit rate is the proportion of all individuals who are correctly assigned by the discriminant functions. The matrix indicates the predictive ability of the discriminant functions with respect to each cluster.

You can also see the mean of each needs variable in each cluster and the mean of each descriptor variable (if you had selected **Discrimination** in the **Set Up** box).

```
Marketing Engineering  Application - [Diagnostic: Segmentation Analysis (PDA)]          _□X
File  Edit  Model  SetUp  Run  Results  View  Window  Help                              _|Ø|X|
□ ☞ ■  ╳ ▣ ▣  ⚇ ? № 🔳 N

Means for each variable in each cluster:

Variable    Overall      CL1          CL2          CL3          CL4          CL5
----------  -----------  -----------  -----------  -----------  -----------  -----------
Innovator    3.63         1.77         3.60         5.82         3.25         2.93
Use_Pager    3.46         2.15         4.70         3.65         4.88         1.86
Use_Phone    3.72         4.69         2.30         4.53         2.25         4.71
Use_Schdl    3.89         3.77         3.00         5.35         2.25         4.43
Inf_Passiv   3.56         1.62         3.85         2.65         5.63         4.86
Inf_Active   4.01         2.38         3.95         4.53         5.13         4.36
Remote_Loc   4.50         4.54         4.80         3.88         5.00         4.50
Wireless     2.90         1.46         5.10         1.65         5.25         1.29
Share_Inf    3.40         3.38         3.10         2.47         5.75         3.64
Monthly      20.3        12.7         31.0         10.9         40.6         11.8
Invoice      993.        527.         755.         .159E+04     .191E+04     521.

For Help, press F1
```

EXHIBIT 7

Once you settle on a solution you may wish to name the clusters for identification and for generating reports. Choose names that seem to best characterize those clusters. On the **Edit** menu click **Edit Cluster Labels** and enter the appropriate names in the boxes provided.

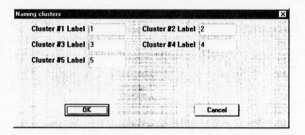

Once you complete cluster analysis, you can use the results of the completed analysis to classify any number of new cases according to the discriminant functions. This ability to assign a large database of customers to selected target segments based on a smaller study sample enhances the implementability of the segmentation study. First, load a file containing demographic information about the new cases. For the purposes of this tutorial you may use PDA_DIS.DAT for classification. Go to the **File** menu and click **Load Classify**.

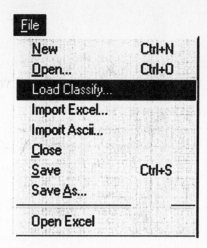

Next, go to the **Run** menu and click **Classify**.

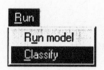

This will display the results of the classification analysis on the spreadsheet, showing the segment to which each new case was assigned. Here case 1 is assigned to cluster 1, case 3 to cluster 2, etc.

	Age	Education	Income	Construc	mergenc	Sales	Service	Professn
1 => 1	32.0	3.0	20.0	0.0	0.0	0.0	0.0	0.0
2 => 2	42.0	3.0	47.0	0.0	0.0	0.0	1.0	0.0
3 => 2	22.0	3.0	28.0	0.0	0.0	0.0	1.0	0.0
4 => 1	46.0	2.0	45.0	0.0	0.0	1.0	0.0	0.0
5 => 2	54.0	2.0	51.0	0.0	0.0	0.0	1.0	0.0
6 => 3	25.0	4.0	81.0	0.0	0.0	0.0	0.0	1.0
7 => 4	46.0	1.0	25.0	1.0	0.0	0.0	0.0	0.0
8 => 3	33.0	3.0	42.0	0.0	0.0	0.0	0.0	1.0
9 => 5	35.0	4.0	30.0	0.0	0.0	0.0	0.0	1.0
10 => 1	51.0	1.0	41.0	0.0	0.0	1.0	0.0	0.0

Marketing Engineering Application - [Data: Targeting analysis (PDA)]

File Edit Model Set Up Run Results View Window Help

For Help, press F1

Limitations of the educational version of the software

Maximum number of variables: 15
Maximum number of observations: 200
Maximum number of clusters: 9
Nominal variables: Cannot use nominal data in cluster analysis, but you could use nominal variables (dummy coded) in discriminant analysis.

References

Dillon, William R. and Goldstein, Matthew 1984, *Multivariate Analysis: Methods and Applications*, John Wiley & Sons, New York.

Hartigan, J.A. and Wong, M. A. 1979, "K-Means Algorithm," *Applied Statistics*, Vol. 28, No. 1, pp. 100-108.

Lilien, Gary L. and Rangaswamy, Arvind 1998, *Marketing Engineering: Computer-Assisted Marketing Analysis and Planning*, Chapter 3, Addison Wesley Longman, Reading, Massachusetts.

Moriarty, Rowland T. and Reibstein, David J. 1982, *Benefit Segmentation: An Industrial Application*, Report No. 82-110, Marketing Science Institute, Cambridge, Massachusetts.

Murtagh, F. 1985, *Multidimensional Clustering Algorithms* (CompStat Lectures 4), Physica-Verlag, Würzburg/Wien.

Ward, J. 1963 "Hierarchical Grouping to Optimize an Objective Function," *Journal of the American Statistical Association,* Vol. 58, pp. 236-244.

CONGLOMERATE INC'S NEW PDA CASE

Conglomerate Inc.'s new PDA (1995)

The cellular phone division of Conglomerate Inc. has teamed up with a PC manufacturer to develop, produce, and market a novel hybrid combination of a personal digital assistant (PDA) and a "smart" cellular phone. They have tentatively named it **ConneCtor**. It transmits and receives both data and voice (unlike competing PDAs which focus on data).

ConneCtor
Another Conglomerate Success Story?

ConneCtor is lightweight and is shaped like a portable phone with a small backlit LCD touch screen along the handset. Its (open) operating system performs standard cellphone functions and such personal information management (PIM) functions as a calendar, calculator, and address book. It can send and receive faxes, voice messages, and e-mail. Users can input data in four ways:

- By typing on the screen keyboard
- By using a numerical keyboard
- By writing on the screen in "digital ink"
- By speaking into the phone (it includes voice recognition software)

The voice recognition feature is based on a neural network that is trained to recognize a particular user's voice patterns. An additional feature unique to **ConneCtor** is linkage via wireless local area networks to other PDA's.

In summary, the features of Conglomerate's handheld device are:

- Instant communication from PDA to PDA
- Cellular phone and pager, fax and e-mail
- Calendar, scheduler, calculator, and address book
- An open system for customized applications
- A paperless note pad
- Voice recognition

Conglomerate is now trying to identify segments within the market for PDAs, target appropriate segment(s) for **ConneCtor,** and position **ConneCtor** in the chosen segments.

Background on the PDA market

In August 1993, Apple introduced its Newton PDA. The broad acceptance that Apple had anticipated did not materialize, and Apple sold only 80,000 Newtons that year. In 1995, the PDA appeared to be on the verge of greater growth and development. The PDA market had grown in four areas: specialized vertical applications (e.g., physician scheduling), PIM (Personal Information Management), mobile communications, and as a supplementary gateway into the Internet.

Even though it has four main applications, the PDA is primarily targeted at "road warriors" or "mobile professionals." This group consists of approximately 25 million people in the United States, of whom about 5 million travel with a computer notebook. Many of these individuals already have cellular phones and must send and receive a large number of messages and data. The standard PDA cannot handle their needs.

The survey

Conglomerate, Inc. hired a market research firm to survey the market across a broad range of occupation types. The survey includes a screening item asking respondents if they had or would consider a

PDA. Only those respondents who answered affirmatively to that question were retained for further analysis.

The questionnaire

The questionnaire asked the respondents to provide data on two kinds of variables: segmentation basis or needs variables and variables that could be used in describing or targeting the clusters using discriminant analysis.

Questions for determining segmentation-basis variables

X1   Whenever new technologies emerge in my field, I am among the first to adopt them.
    (1 = Strongly disagree......7 = Strongly agree)
How often do you use the following:
    (1 = Never......7 = Always)

X2   a. Pager?

X3   b. Phone or voice mail?

X4   c. Scheduling or contact-management tools, i.e., filofax or similar devices?

X5   How often do others send you time-sensitive information (e.g., work orders)?
    (1 = Never......7 = Daily)

X6   How often do you have to send time-sensitive information while away from your office?
    (1 = Never ...... 7 = Daily)

X7   How much of your time do you spend away from your office location?
    (1 = 0 %......7 = 70% or more)

X8   How important is wireless communication to you?
    (1 = Not at all important.....7 = Very important)

X9   How important is it for you to share information rapidly with colleagues while away from an office location?
    (1 = Not at all important......7 = Very important)
How much would you be willing to pay for a personal digital assistant (PDA) with the following features: instant communication from PDA to PDA, cellular phone and pager, fax and e-mail, calendar, scheduler, calculator, address book, open system for customized applications, paperless note pad, and voice recognition?

X10   a. Monthly (for all services that you use)?

X11   b. Invoice price for the PDA device with all features?

Questions for determining variables for discriminant analysis

Z1   Age
Z2   Education (1 = High school, 2 = Some college, 3 = College, 4 = Graduate degree)
Z3   Income

Type of industry or occupation:
     (0 = No, 1 = Yes)
Z4   Construction
Z5   Emergency (fire, police, ambulance, etc.)
Z6   Sales (insurance, pharmacy, etc.)
Z7   Maintenance and service
Z8   Professional (e.g., lawyer, consultant, etc.)
Z9   Do you own a PDA?

Media consumption (Readership of magazines):
     (0 = No, 1 = Yes)
Z10   *Businessweek*
Z11   *PC Magazine*
Z12   *Field & Stream*
Z13   *Modern Gourmet*

EXERCISES

1. Run only cluster analysis (without **Discrimination**) on the data to try to identify the number of distinct segments present in this market. Consider both the distances separating the segments and the characteristics of the resulting segments.

2. Identify and profile (name) the clusters that you select. Given the attributes of **ConneCtor**, which cluster would you target for your marketing campaign?

3. Go back to **Set Up**, check **Discrimination**, and rerun the analysis. How would you go about targeting the segment(s) you picked in question 2?

4. How has this analysis helped you to segment the market for **ConneCtor**?

5. What other analyses would you do to develop a marketing program for **ConneCtor**? Indicate both the type of data you would collect (if any) and the types of analyses you would conduct.

Chapter 2

TUTORIAL FOR THE GE PORTFOLIO PLANNING MODEL (GE)

Concept

The idea behind the GE/McKinsey approach is to evaluate each business unit along two composite dimensions: industry attractiveness and business strength. These dimensions, in turn, are composed of a series of weighted factors. Both the factor weights and the factors themselves may vary from one application to another, for example, industry attractiveness includes measures of market size, growth rate, competitive intensity and the like while business strength normally includes such measures as market share, share growth and product quality. Management then gives each business a rating for each factor and gives each factor a weight. These factor ratings are multiplied by the weights and summed to arrive at a position in the strength/attractiveness matrix.

The matrix has nine cells and the three in the upper right are those in which the company has a strong position and would be considered for investment and growth. The three along the diagonal are of intermediate attractiveness and the company should consider a policy selectively enhancing business in those cells to generate earnings. And finally the three cells in the lower left corner are low in overall attractiveness and the company should consider harvesting and divesting businesses in those cells.

Software

To run the GE model, select the **Model** menu, choose **GE: Portfolio Planning** (ge.xls) and then **Generalized Model** to see the **Introduction** screen.

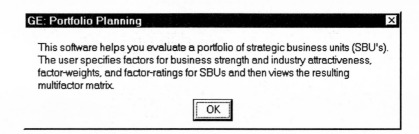

Click **OK** to get to the main worksheet, which will prompt you for your input.

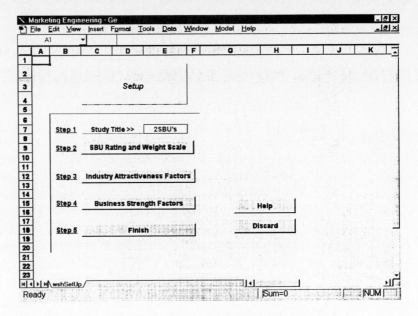

As an example, set up a simple problem consisting of two SBUs. Provide a study title and click **SBU rating and Weight Scale** to advance to the next screen and set up the model.

You will be asked to enter the minimum and the maximum value for SBU ratings and Weights. (The software will check to see that your input values fall within these ranges). Once you have entered those values, click **OK**

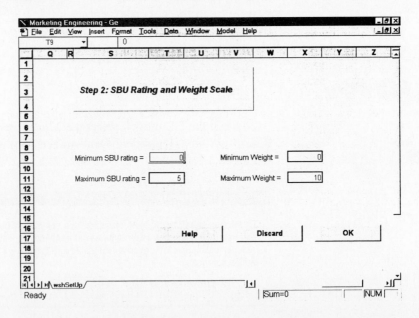

For step 3, select **Industry Attractiveness Factors**. Choose the industry attractiveness dimensions on which the SBUs will be evaluated. Some prospective factors are listed. Click each item in the list that you wish to include and then click **Add,** and the program will include it in your analysis. (Note: the items with a " C# " after them refer to the factors defined by Cooper, (1993, p. 310)).

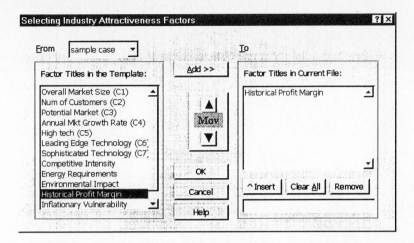

You can also add your own dimensions indicating industry attractiveness. In this example we added the item "Global opportunities" to the list by entering it in the bottom right area and clicking the **Insert** button. If you are dissatisfied with a selection you can highlight an item and click **Remove** or you can **Clear All**.

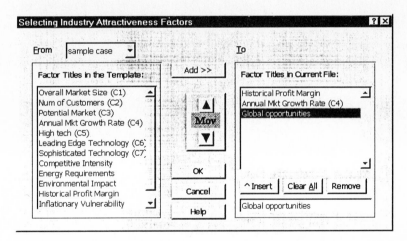

Click **OK** to get back to the initial set-up screen. For step 4, click **Business Strength Factors**. (Again, the items with a " C# " after them refer to the factors defined by Cooper, (1993, p. 310)).

Now you need to list the factors that serve as indicators of business strength. Choose from Factor Titles in the Template using **Add** or enter your own factors in the lower right area using **Insert** as you did with the Industry Attractiveness factors. Click **OK** when you are finished.

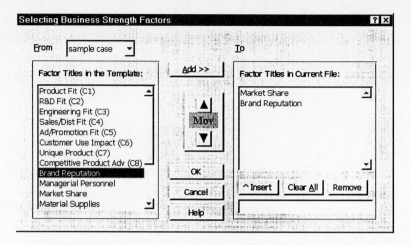

Again click **OK** to get back to the initial set-up screen. Once you have finished the initial set up, click **Finish** (step 5) to continue or select **Discard**.

If you choose **Finish**, the system will customize the worksheet according to your setup and then prompt you for a file name under which to save your basic model setup.

Generally it is a good idea to save your newly configured model now. Give it a name other than GE.xls.

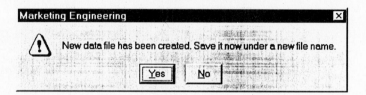

Now you are set to assess the SBUs of interest on the basis of the dimensions you just specified. The following screen shows the **Main Menu** for the evaluation task.

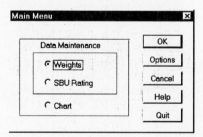

First select **Weights** to indicate the importance weights for each of the factors you chose. The weights are multipliers of the SBU item ratings you will set subsequently.

NOTE: *These are relative weights, so giving every item a '1' is the same as giving every item a '2'.*

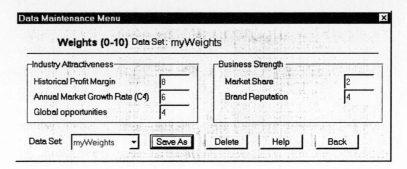

Click **Save As** to save your weights for future use. You can define multiple sets of importance weights, saving each under a different name.

Click **Back** to get back to the **Main Menu**. Next choose **SBU Rating**.

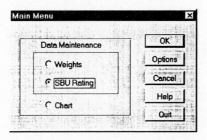

Rate the first SBU on the Industry Attractiveness and Business Strength dimensions and save these by clicking **Save As**.

NOTE: *The rating for Sales Potential does not affect the location of the SBU in the GE matrix, but it will determine the size of the circles in the resulting chart.*

Repeat the procedure to include other SBUs for analysis. Click **Back** to go back to the **Main Menu**.

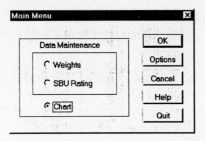

Finally select **Chart** and click **OK**. You will see an empty Multi-factor Portfolio Matrix.

To see the result for your input, load the rating information about the SBUs into the chart by clicking **Add from Database**.

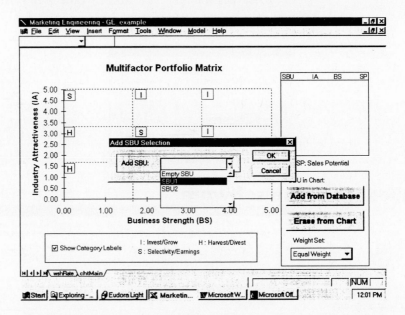

You can test what happens when you apply different weighting schemes, e.g., customized weights versus equal weights (a set of weights that are included as a default option). If different managers weight the factors differently, it can be a very valuable exercise to examine the strategic consequences of those differences.

Strategy implications for individual SBUs can be drawn from their positioning on the matrix, as indicated by the category labels. For example SBU 1 belongs to the category "H" standing for Harvest and Divest.

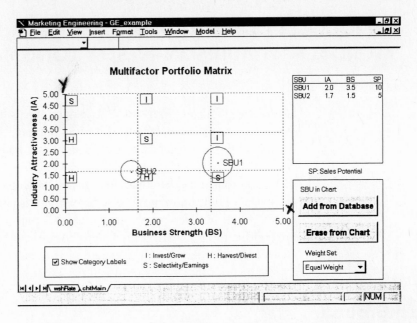

If you need to make changes or additions to the weight sets or the SBU rating sets, go to **Model** in the main menu bar and choose **Main Menu**.

Limitations of the software

Maximum number of industry attractiveness indicators:	15
Maximum number of business strength indicators:	15
Maximum number of cases plotted in chart:	10

References

Cooper, Robert G. 1993, *Winning at New Products*, second edition, Addison Wesley Longman, Reading, Massachusetts, p. 310.

Wind, Yoram; Mahajan, Vijay; and Swire, Donald J. 1983, "An Empirical Comparison of Standardized Portfolio Models," *Journal of Marketing*, Vol. 47, No. 2 (Spring), pp. 89-99.

PRODUCT PLANNING USING THE GE/McKINSEY APPROACH AT ADDISON WESLEY LONGMAN CASE*

It was July 1997 and Mark Roth, manager of business books at Addison Wesley Longman, was facing a bit of a dilemma. He was about to present his 1998 fiscal year new book budget and had three new marketing books in his portfolio. One of them, *Marketing Engineering*, was a bit different from the other two. It did not currently have a large natural market but might ultimately be a big winner, he thought, if it were promoted properly. He was about to make his plans for annual promotion, kicking his program off at the August American Marketing Association Educator's Conference in Chicago. His main question was—How should he prioritize the promotional resources for the three new books?

Background

Addison Wesley Longman is one of the largest global educational publishers, selling books, multimedia and learning programs in all major academic disciplines to the primary, secondary, higher education, professional and English language teaching markets throughout the world.

AWL is part of the Pearson Group. Pearson plc, headquartered in London, is an international provider of media content and is comprised of information, education and entertainment companies. Pearson reported the following fiscal year-end figures:

1996 Sales ($ mil.): $3,746.8
1-Yr. Sales Growth: 19.5%

1996 Net Inc. ($ mil.): $413.1
1-Yr. Net Inc. Growth: (7.7%)

1996 Employees: 17,383
1-Yr. Employee Growth: (10.5%)

In addition to AWL, some of their companies include: the Financial Times Newspaper, Penguin/Putnam, The Economist Group (50%), Pearson Professional, and Pearson Television. In 1988, Addison-Wesley was acquired by Pearson plc. The Company merged with Longman, a sister Pearson publisher, in 1995 and became Addison Wesley Longman. In 1996, AWL acquired HarperCollins Educational Publishers, consisting

---

* Note: The individuals, events and details in this case are fictional and were created purely for pedagogic purposes. The background about AWL and the three books is real, however.

of HarperCollins College and Scott Foresman, and merged those operations with AWL's.

Each company that makes up AWL has historic publishing strengths and accomplishments. Many people in the U.S. remember learning to read with Elson Basic Readers featuring Dick, Jane and Spot. Scott Foresman, their publisher, celebrated its centennial in 1996. Longman, which published Dr. Samuel Johnson and Wordsworth, among other British literary lights, has a distinguished 273-year tradition. The former HarperCollins College, now part of the Higher Education Publishing Group, traces its roots back to 1817 when the brothers Harper established a publishing house in New York City. When Melbourne Wesley Cummings published MIT physics professor Francis Sears' *Mechanics* in 1942, Addison-Wesley was launched as an outstanding publisher of science, mathematics and computer texts.

The college division of AWL markets books to colleges and universities throughout the world. Its main promotional resources are sampling, brochures, direct mail, exhibitions (primarily at academic meetings) and direct selling to professors. The US college division salesforce includes over 200 individuals, each of whom specializes in an academic specialty (business, science, humanities) and works in a regional territory, servicing several dozen schools. AWL believes that its salesforce is particularly important in encouraging instructors to consider and adopt new textbooks, and they use their salesforce as a key tool in their product introduction mix.

The New Marketing Texts:

The three new marketing texts that AWL was introducing in the summer of 1997 were:

> *Advertising and Sales Promotion Strategy* by Gerry Tellis, USC, aimed primarily at MBA adverting and sales promotion courses;

> *Analysis for Strategic Marketing* by Vithala R. Rao, Cornell University and Joel H. Steckel, New York University, aimed at capstone MBA strategic marketing courses, particularly those with analytic content; and

> *Marketing Engineering* by Gary L. Lilien and Arvind Rangaswamy, Penn State, a book and extensive package of software to deliver marketing tools to support marketing decision making.

The *Marketing Engineering* book was a bit different from others in that it included two volumes plus a CD with 26 software packages that could be applied immediately to both classroom and prototype professional business problems. However, as the book was sufficiently different from anything else on the market, both Mark and the authors felt that that AWL selling effort could make a critical difference in the acceptance of the book, especially in the short run.

The New Marketing Book Promotional Challenge:

As Mark was finalizing his proposal, he began glancing through the *Marketing Engineering* book. He noticed that the book identified several methods that could be used to approach a problem just like his.

"What a novel idea," he thought. "Why not use ideas and tools from *Marketing Engineering* to help determine what to do here."

He determined that one Marketing Engineering tool might be appropriate for his problem: the GE/McKinsey approach.

Applying the GE Approach:

Mark found the GE approach implemented in *Marketing Engineering* in a tool called Portfolio Planning (GE). In consultation with his planning staff, Mark came up with the following factors for the components of the composite dimensions:

Industry Attractiveness:

Market Size (total volume of books to be sold in the next three years).
Growth rate (annual growth rate of market size).
Technological requirements[**] (high would be "traditional book," low would include need for capabilities of producing multimedia, software, etc.).
Leading edge[**] (low would include more traditional topics; high would include new and emerging topics).

Business Strength:

Market share (book's likely share of market after two to three years).
Share growth (annual growth rate of market share).
Investment/cost[**] (high means low need for investment; low means high need for investment).
Synergy (ability of book to induce sales of other AW books or to lead to signings of new authors).

Mark then attempted to assign weights (from 1 to 5) to the factors above. He decided that the weights depended on the strategic position of the firm—whether it wanted to view itself more traditionally or leading edge. Hence he constructed two sets of weights: "Traditional," and "Leading Edge" (Exhibit 1). He also rated each of the businesses, Tellis, Rao/Steckel and L&R on each of the factors (Exhibit 2).

[**] Note: Because of the way the GE approach works, "high" means better for the firm, "low" means worse. So, "high cost" gets a low rating and "low cost" gets a high rating.

	Traditional Weights	Leading Edge Weights
Industry Attractiveness		
Market size	5	2
Growth rate	2	5
Technological requirements	5	1
Leading edge	1	5
Business Strength		
Market share	3	2
Share growth	1	5
Investment/cost	5	1
Synergy	1	5

EXHIBIT 1
AWL's weights for new marketing texts (1-5 scale).

	Tellis	Rao/Steckel	Lilien/ Rangaswamy
Sales Potential	20	15	12
Industry Attrativeness			
Market size	5	3	2
Growth rate	2	4	4
Technological requirements	4	5	1
Leading edge	2	3	5
Business Strength			
Market share	3	2	2
Share growth	3	4	4
Investment/cost	4	5	1
Synergy	1	3	5

EXHIBIT 2
Ratings for new AWL marketing texts.

The Problem:

Mark was planning to allocate his new product budget equally across the books. Using the GE approach:

1. Describe the business portfolio and the options available to AWL
2. What does the GE approach suggest about the relationship between AWL's strategic objectives and its promotional plans?
3. What should Mark do?
4. What other considerations emerge in setting and allocating the budget?
5. Comment on the uses and limitations of the GE model.

APPENDIX
Details of the Three Books from AWL's Web Site

1. ***Advertising and Sales Promotion Strategy***

First Edition, 475 pages, 1998, Cloth

Gerard J. Tellis, University of Southern California

Unique; theoretically rigorous, rich with examples, and useful for designing successful strategies.

Promotion is a rich topic that integrates perspectives from a number of disciplines including marketing, economics, psychology, anthropology, and operations research. It is also a dynamic area that is constantly changing as firms develop new media, appeals, and methods to better compete with their rivals in a rapidly changing environment. Advertising and Promotional Strategy is designed to communicate all of these aspects of promotion. After reading this book, prospective managers will understand the topic of promotion well enough to be able to design successful strategies.

Hallmark Features

Tellis' writing is simple, direct, and lively. He uses short sentences and simple language even when explaining complex ideas.

The text has a managerial orientation—more so than any other text in the field—helping prospective managers understand the topic well enough to design successful strategies.

The book's presentation is practical, analyzing a large number of relevant examples and describing creative promotional strategies.

Tellis draws from the most recent research in the social sciences to ensure that students are exposed to the most current knowledge in the field.

This book explains why phenomena occur and tries to show why certain strategies succeed, while others fail. Using contemporary examples, the author clearly communicates points.

Tellis explains theories, concepts and terms from first principles—his book requires no particular prerequisites in business, marketing, economics or psychology.

Special topics include coverage of regulation (chapter 2), direct marketing (chapter 16), ethics, international strategy, and brand equity.

Your students will enjoy the text's 16-page color advertisement insert, lavish examples and numerous illustrations.

Supplements include: Instructor's Manual with Test Bank/Transparency Masters/CD-ROM Guide, a Computerized Test Bank for Windows, a Videotape with advertisement clips for classroom use, an Instructor's CD-ROM with ad stills and clips, and an Interactive CD-ROM case on Intel that allows the student to act as a Marketing Manager designing a promotional strategy.

This title has the following supplements:

Instructor's Resource Manual by Siva K. Balasubramanian, Southern Illinois University includes the Instructor's Manual, Test Bank, Transparency Masters, and CD-ROM Guide.

Instructor's CD-ROM includes a gallery of print advertisements and quick-time clips of TV commercials.

Videotape contains advertisement clips for classroom use.

Intel Case CD-ROM, for Windows by John Quelch, Harvard University Business School, is based on a Harvard Case Study on the Advertising Campaign for Intel on introducing their product into the UK market. The student acts as a marketing manager with an advertising budget, who needs to decide to target: the novice home computer buyer, the average business person who uses a computer, or the corporate purchasing person. With this, they then develop an advertising and promotion campaign using a series of provided advertisements, etc. 0-321-02175-4

2. *Analysis for Strategic Marketing*

First Edition, 400 pages, 1998, Paper

Vithala R. Rao, Cornell University
Joel H. Steckel, New York University

Provides more modern scientific marketing methods for strategic marketing courses than any other book on the market.

Analysis for Strategic Marketing is the first book in the market to tie the aspects of strategic marketing and marketing research together. In fact, this book is so unique that it has no direct competitors—it simply fits in a class of its own. Rao and Steckel offer you this paperback book as a versatile tool to be used as a main text or supplement in your Senior undergraduate or MBA-level advanced Marketing Research or Strategic Marketing courses.

Hallmark Features
This text contains a mid- to high-level mixture of strategy and marketing research.
　Adding analysis and research tools to traditional marketing book material, Analysis for Strategic Marketing is considered unique.

Offering four cases with solutions included in the Instructor's Manual, Rao and Steckel allow and encourage flexible use of their textbook.

This title has the following supplements:

Instructor's Manual Package by Marjorie Doyen, Cornell University, includes the Instructor's Manual, Test Bank and Data Disk.

3. ***Marketing Engineering: Computer-Assisted Marketing Analysis and Planning***

First Edition, 400 pages, 1998, Paper

Gary L. Lilien, Penn State and Arvind Rangaswamy, Penn State

This book integrates concepts, analytic marketing techniques, and operational software to train the new generation of marketers, helping them to become marketing engineers.

This textbook and the related course are aimed at educating and training marketing engineers to translate concepts into context-specific operational approaches using analytical, quantitative, and computer modeling techniques. As an underlying philosophy, this book links theory to practice and practice to theory. The entire textbook package is made up of three components: the main text; a CD-ROM that includes 26 software packages as well as customized on-line help files; and a user manual which contains software tutorials, problem sets, and cases that enable the student to apply the concepts and software, providing them with an immediate learning experience. Lilien and Rangaswamy designed this primarily as a text for a one-semester, capstone MBA course, but the material has been used successfully in executive programs and in undergraduate classes as well.

Hallmark Features

This book is so cutting-edge—integrating concepts, analytic marketing techniques, and operational software—that it has no direct competition.

The text material provides a detailed, but user-oriented view of the marketing engineering approach to marketing problems in the information age.

Chapter summaries highlight key points in each chapter while problem sets and cases enable students to apply the concepts and software.

This book is uniquely packaged as three components: Text, User Manual, and CD-ROM. The 26 software packages on the CD-ROM allow students to implement the concepts in the course and to apply those concepts immediately—each package includes a customized set of on-line help files. The User Manual includes problem sets and cases, as well as a tutorial for each software package with step-by-step instructions.

The videotape, available to adopters, provides award-winning examples of how concepts and tools and have been applied profitably in a number of companies, saving them millions or even billions of dollars.

Created by the authors out of Penn State, the book's Web site can be used for problems and for obtaining software updates and upgrades.

This title has the following supplements:

Videotape that provides award-winning examples of how concepts and tools and have been applied profitably in a number of companies, saving them millions or even billions of dollars.

Instructor's Manual/Solutions Manual/Transparency Masters/Instructor's CD-ROM with PP. The Instructor's CD-ROM contains a complete PowerPoint Presentation for the professor to illustrate key concepts in each chapter.

Chapter 3

TUTORIAL FOR POSITIONING ANALYSIS

Concept

There are three broad concepts associated with this tutorial: Differentiation, Positioning, and Mapping. ***Differentiation*** is the creation of tangible or intangible differences on one or two key dimensions between a focal product and its main competitors. ***Positioning*** refers to the set of strategies organizations develop and implement to ensure that these differences occupy a distinct and important position in the minds of customers. Thus, Kentucky Fried Chicken differentiates its chicken products by using a unique blend of spices, cooking vessels, and cooking processes and positions its products as "finger-lickin' good." ***Mapping*** refers to techniques that enable managers to develop differentiation and positioning strategies by helping them to visualize the competitive structure of their markets as perceived by their customers. Typically, data for mapping are customer perceptions of existing products (and new concepts) along various attributes, perceptions of similarities between brands, customer preferences for products, or measures of behavioral response of customers toward the products (e.g., current market shares of the products).

Maps generated by this software are spatial representations in Euclidean space that have the following characteristics: (1) The pairwise distances between product alternatives directly indicate the "perceived similarities" between any pair of products, i.e., how close or far apart the products are in the minds of customers. (2) A vector on the map (shown by a blue or red line) indicates both magnitude and direction in the Euclidean space. The length of a vector indicates its magnitude. A blue vector geometrically denotes product attributes (i.e., direction in which the labeled attribute corresponding to a vector is increasing) and a red vector denotes the direction in which an individual's preferences are increasing. (3) The axes of the map are a special set of vectors that could represent the underlying dimensions that best characterize how customers differentiate between alternatives. One way to interpret the axes is to look for attributes that are most closely correlated with each axis. The smaller the angle between an axis and an attribute, the higher is the correlation.

This software implements the MDPREF perceptual mapping model, which is based on a factor-analytic procedure. In addition, the software implements PREFMAP-3, which enables users to introduce for each respondent a preference-vector onto a given perceptual map. Typically, a perceptual map is derived from the averaged perception data from a target segment, whereas the preference map is derived from individual-level preference data. This two-step procedure, referred to as joint-space mapping with external analysis, is based on the assumption that a target segment has a common set of perceptions among the choice alternatives, but each respondent has different preferences for those alternatives. For example, Volvo may be perceived to be a safe car by all respondents, but only some respondents may have high preference for Volvo.

(Note: All the procedures in this software are based on "vector" methods. Thus, we do not include "ideal-point" or unfolding models.)

Software

The following example illustrates the use of mapping for developing a positioning strategy for Infiniti G20. We describe the data in detail in the exercise.

From the **Model** menu, select **Positioning Analysis**. You will be prompted for a data file. For this example, select the file called G20.DAT. If you enter your own data sets, make sure that the columns are the products (or alternatives to be evaluated) and the rows contain the attribute evaluations of the products.

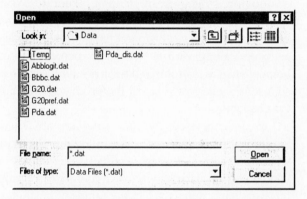

After the file loads, you will see the following split-screen window:

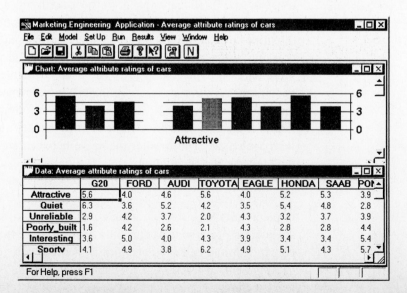

	G20	FORD	AUDI	TOYOTA	EAGLE	HONDA	SAAB	PON
Attractive	5.6	4.0	4.6	5.6	4.0	5.2	5.3	3.9
Quiet	6.3	3.6	5.2	4.2	3.5	5.4	4.8	2.8
Unreliable	2.9	4.2	3.7	2.0	4.3	3.2	3.7	3.9
Poorly_built	1.6	4.2	2.6	2.1	4.3	2.8	2.8	4.4
Interesting	3.6	5.0	4.0	4.3	3.9	3.4	3.4	5.4
Sporty	4.1	4.9	3.8	6.2	4.9	5.1	4.3	5.7

NOTE: *If you make changes to the data to evaluate alternative solutions, the program will not automatically save these changes. To save the changes (under a separate file if necessary) go to the **File** menu and click **Save As**.*

On the **Set Up** menu, click **Setup** to select the parameters for the run.

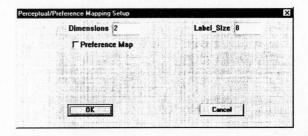

Number of dimensions: Enter either 2 or 3. If you choose a three-dimensional map, the program will produce three two-dimensional maps (Dim 1 with Dim 2; Dim1 with Dim 3, and Dim2 with Dim3).

Label Size: Because long labels might clutter the map(s), you can control the length of labels in the map by specifying between one and 10 characters.

Perceptual Map: This is the default option. For input it relies on customers' average perceptions of a set of alternatives on a set of attributes. For this exercise the data is contained in the file G20.DAT. Although this default option generates only perceptual maps and not joint-space maps (containing both perceptions and preferences), you can still obtain simple joint-space maps by including the average preference ratings in your input data matrix.

Preference Map: Select the preference map option if you have a separate file containing information on the preferences of each customer for the selected products. For the G20 exercise, the preference data are contained in the file called G20PREF.DAT. If you choose **Preference Map** you will be prompted to provide this file name.

To run the program, go to the **Run** menu and click **Run Model**.

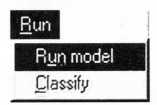

When the program is successfully executed, you will see the following map on the top part of your screen.

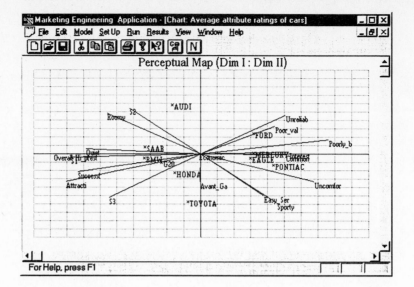

In the map, the length of an attribute vector is proportional to the variance of that attribute explained by the map.

Go to the **View** menu to find commands to customize the display. You have the following choices:

1. ***Zooming in and out***: Use the Zoom command to enlarge any portion of the display. First click **Zoom In**, and then place the cursor anywhere on the map and click. To zoom out again, go back to the **View** menu and click **Zoom Out**.

2. ***Customize the display***: On the **View** menu, click **View Options** to customize the display:

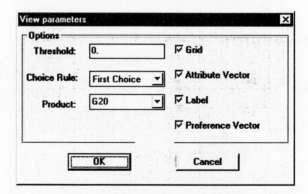

   - Turn the grid on or off.
   - Turn the display of attribute vectors on or off.
   - Display only attributes whose variance recovery is higher than a specified number. Select the threshold values from 0 (default) to 1.0.
   - If you choose to turn off the display of both attribute vectors and labels, the program will display only objects (cars in the example).

The remaining options are used with preference maps, which we describe later.

3. ***Add labels anywhere on the map***: This may be useful for future identification of the map. Click anywhere on the map, and a label dialog box will appear. Anything you enter in this dialog box will be inserted at the selected location on the map. To delete the labels you entered, go to the **Edit** menu and choose **Delete Labels**.

To print a copy of the map on an attached printer, go to the **File** menu and click **Print**. To cut and paste the map into a Windows application (e.g., Word for Windows), bring the map to the foreground, go to the **Edit** menu and select **Cut** or **Copy** and then bring a Windows application to the foreground, go to the **Edit** menu, and select **Paste**.

In the case of 3-D maps, the program displays automatically only a map of dimensions 1 and 2. To view the other dimensions on the **Results** menu, choose **Summary** and then **View Next Chart** as shown below.

Alternatively, click on the  button on the Menu Bar to view the next chart.

Preference maps

If you chose **Preference Map** in the **Setup** menu, the map will include the preference vectors of each individual shown as red lines. The length of a preference vector is proportional to the variance of that respondent's preferences that are explained by the map.

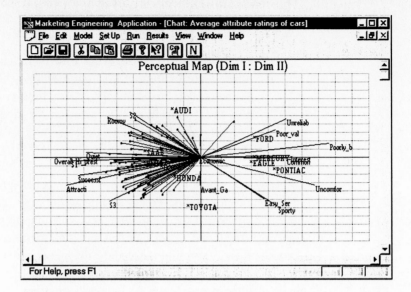

Customize the viewing and analysis options: As with the perceptual map, you can use the options under the **View** menu to customize the display. You will have some new options that were not available with perceptual maps. Go to **View** and choose **View Options.** You can use these options to:

- Turn the display of the preference vectors on or off.
- Select a product whose market share you would like to explore at various locations on the map.
- Select the choice rule to be used for market-share computations. Under the first-choice rule, we assume that each customer will purchase only his or her most preferred product. Under the share-of-preference rule, we assume that the probability that a customer will select a product is proportional to the product's share of preference with respect to all the products included in the model.

NOTE: *The share-of-preference model, as implemented here, arbitrarily sets the preference value of a customer's least preferred product to 0.*

To compute an index of market share at any location on the map for a selected product, place the cursor anywhere on the map and click the **right mouse button**. Cross hairs will appear at that position on the map, along with a market-share figure (at the bottom of the screen) as shown below. It is best to interpret the computed market share as a measure of the *relative attractiveness* (relative to market share at the original position) of the selected location on the map for the selected product, rather than as an indicator of the absolute magnitude of the market share that will be realized.

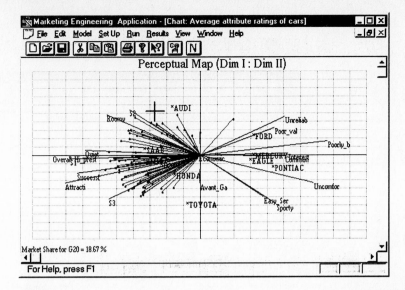

NOTE: *In computing market share, we assume that the selected product is relocated to the new position shown by the cross hairs (the map will still show the selected product at its original location for purposes of comparison), while all other products remain at their original positions.*

To view additional information of a diagnostic nature, go to the **Results** menu and select **View Diagnostics**. This produces a display of additional information useful in evaluating the statistical adequacy of the generated map. You can print this information to an attached printer by going to the **File** menu and selecting **Print**, or use the Windows cut-and-paste option to copy this information into another Windows application, such as Word for Windows, for further editing.

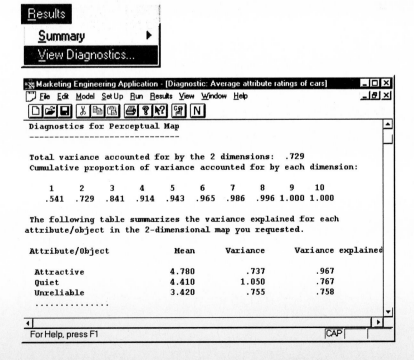

If you had checked **Preference Map** in the **Set Up** menu, you will get additional diagnostics as shown in the screen below:

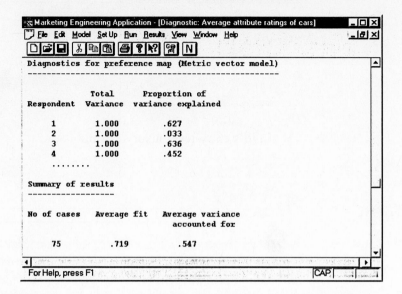

References

Green, Paul E. and Wind, Yoram 1973, *Multiattribute Decisions in Marketing: A Measurement Approach,* The Dryden Press, Hinsdale, Illinois.

Green, Paul E.; Carmone, Frank J., Jr.; and Smith, Scott M. 1989, *Multidimensional Scaling: Concepts and Application,* Allyn and Bacon, Boston, Massachusetts.

Muelman, Jacqueline; Heiser, Wilhelm; and Carroll, J. Douglas 1986, *PREFMAP-3 User's Guide,* Bell Laboratories, Murray Hill, New Jersey 07974.

POSITIONING THE INFINITI G20 CASE*

Introducing the G20

In April 1990, Nissan's Infiniti division planned to introduce the G20 in the U.S., adding a third model to the existing Infiniti line. The G20 was already available in Europe and Japan under the name Primera. The car, equipped with a four-cylinder engine developing 140 horsepower, would be Infiniti's entry-level luxury car. Initial market response to the G20 in the U.S. was disappointing, and management wondered how it might retarget or reposition the car to improve its market performance.

Background

In 1989, three years after Honda first introduced its Acura line, Toyota and Nissan attacked the U.S. luxury car market, a segment previously dominated by American and German manufacturers.

In November 1989, Nissan launched its new luxury Infiniti division with the $40,000 Q45 as its lead car and the $20,000 M30. However Nissan was somewhat late: In August 1989, three months before Nissan shipped its first Infiniti, Toyota had introduced Lexus, its luxury brand with a two-car line comprising the $40,000 LS400 and the entry-level LS250.

As the figures for January to September 1990 showed, Lexus outsold Infiniti by 50,000 to 15,000. The reasons for Infiniti's slow start were threefold.

- First the Infiniti Q45 came to the market after the Lexus LS400 had established a good market position.
- Second Lexus had two very good cars, whereas Infiniti's M30 coupe received poor evaluations from the automobile press and from customers.
- Finally the eccentric Infiniti advertising campaign that showed scenes of nature, but not the car itself, shared some of the blame. ("Infiniti may not be doing so well, but, hey, at least sales of rocks and trees are skyrocketing," commented comedian Jay Leno.)

Research data

Exhibits 1–4 summarize some of the data that Infiniti had in early 1990. Data in Exhibits 1 and 2 are based on a survey of customers from its target segments, described as people between 25 and 35 with annual

---

* This case was developed by Katrin Starke and Arvind Rangaswamy and describes a real situation using hypothetical data.

household incomes between $50,000 and $100,000 (when the survey was administered, the Lexus LS250 was not yet well known to the respondents to be included in the study). The three sub-segments in Exhibit 1 (denoted S1, S2, and S3) are based on information provided by Infiniti managers. Exhibit 3 is derived from sales brochures describing the characteristics of each car. Exhibit 4 summarizes demographic and psychographic information about the three sub-segments and was compiled from databases supplied by Claritas, Inc.

	G20	Ford T-bird	Audi 90	Toyota Supra	Eagle Talon	Honda Prelude	Saab 900	Pontiac Firebird	BMW 318i	Mercury Capri
Attractive	5.6	4.0	4.6	5.6	4.0	5.2	5.3	3.9	5.7	3.9
Quiet	6.3	3.6	5.2	4.2	3.5	5.4	4.8	2.8	5.0	3.3
Unreliable	2.9	4.2	3.7	2.0	4.3	3.2	3.7	3.9	2.3	4.0
Poorly Built	1.6	4.2	2.6	2.1	4.3	2.8	2.8	4.4	1.8	4.3
Interesting	3.6	5.0	4.0	4.3	3.9	3.4	3.4	5.4	3.3	3.9
Sporty	4.1	4.9	3.8	6.2	4.9	5.1	4.3	5.7	4.1	5.2
Uncomfortable	2.4	4.0	2.4	3.7	4.0	3.3	2.8	4.3	3.5	4.4
Roomy	5.6	3.9	5.3	3.5	3.6	3.9	5.1	3.3	4.3	3.6
Easy Service	4.6	4.9	3.5	4.9	4.6	5.0	3.8	4.7	4.1	4.6
High Prestige	5.4	3.5	5.6	5.3	2.8	4.7	5.7	3.8	6.4	3.3
Common	3.5	3.6	3.4	2.9	4.3	3.9	1.9	4.3	2.8	3.9
Economical	3.6	3.7	3.6	3.2	4.9	5.0	4.3	3.1	4.3	4.6
Successful	5.3	4.2	5.0	5.5	3.7	5.6	5.3	4.4	5.9	3.9
Avant-garde	4.3	3.6	3.6	4.9	4.4	3.9	4.7	4.1	3.7	4.5
Poor Value	3.4	4.3	4.3	3.5	3.6	2.6	2.9	4.3	3.3	3.8
Preferences										
Overall	6.3	3.9	6.0	5.5	4.0	6.5	6.8	3.0	6.7	4.0
Segment I (S1)	4.3	2.1	6.0	6.1	3.3	6.0	7.5	1.2	8.3	1.7
Segment II (S2)	5.9	6.0	7.7	3.5	3.1	5.5	5.4	2.5	5.4	5.8
Segment III (S3)	8.4	2.1	3.4	8.1	5.8	8.3	8.4	5.3	7.3	3.4

EXHIBIT 1
Survey results with average perception and average preference ratings on a scale from 1 to 9 (G20.DAT).

EXHIBIT 2

Individual-level preference data, measured on a scale from 1 to 9, with higher numbers representing increased preference (GEOPREF.DAT).

	G20	Ford T-bird	Audi 90	Toyota Supra	Eagle Talon	Honda Prelude	Saab 900	Pontiac Firebird	BMW 318i	Mercury Capri
1	4.0	7.0	8.0	3.0	4.0	5.0	5.0	1.0	4.0	5.0
2	4.0	8.0	6.0	5.0	8.0	7.0	3.0	1.0	5.0	2.0
3	8.0	5.0	9.0	4.0	1.0	7.0	7.0	2.0	4.0	4.0
4	7.0	1.0	8.0	1.0	4.0	6.0	5.0	5.0	7.0	3.0
5	8.0	8.0	8.0	3.0	5.0	4.0	3.0	2.0	8.0	6.0
6	5.0	6.0	5.0	5.0	2.0	4.0	8.0	4.0	4.0	7.0
7	3.0	9.0	7.0	4.0	4.0	3.0	6.0	4.0	3.0	6.0
8	4.0	7.0	9.0	3.0	1.0	7.0	9.0	3.0	6.0	6.0
9	8.0	6.0	6.0	4.0	5.0	5.0	1.0	2.0	8.0	7.0
10	6.0	4.0	6.0	3.0	2.0	8.0	7.0	3.0	1.0	8.0
11	8.0	6.0	8.0	4.0	6.0	8.0	7.0	1.0	2.0	7.0
12	8.0	5.0	6.0	6.0	2.0	3.0	8.0	1.0	6.0	6.0
13	4.0	2.0	9.0	4.0	1.0	5.0	5.0	4.0	8.0	5.0
14	5.0	5.0	8.0	5.0	6.0	4.0	6.0	1.0	3.0	7.0
15	6.0	5.0	9.0	1.0	3.0	6.0	8.0	3.0	6.0	3.0
16	6.0	3.0	9.0	2.0	7.0	8.0	6.0	3.0	7.0	3.0
17	8.0	5.0	8.0	1.0	1.0	8.0	9.0	2.0	5.0	4.0
18	5.0	9.0	7.0	5.0	2.0	4.0	7.0	5.0	6.0	1.0
19	6.0	7.0	9.0	6.0	2.0	6.0	3.0	5.0	4.0	5.0
20	6.0	9.0	8.0	2.0	3.0	8.0	6.0	1.0	7.0	5.0
21	7.0	7.0	9.0	4.0	1.0	3.0	4.0	1.0	4.0	3.0
22	6.0	9.0	6.0	2.0	3.0	4.0	6.0	1.0	6.0	3.0
23	5.0	4.0	8.0	4.0	1.0	4.0	1.0	1.0	8.0	5.0
24	7.0	4.0	8.0	3.0	2.0	3.0	4.0	6.0	9.0	5.0
25	4.0	9.0	7.0	3.0	1.0	7.0	2.0	1.0	5.0	7.0
26	8.0	2.0	1.0	9.0	4.0	8.0	8.0	5.0	8.0	4.0
27	8.0	6.0	5.0	8.0	4.0	8.0	7.0	7.0	5.0	1.0
28	9.0	1.0	2.0	4.0	9.0	9.0	9.0	4.0	8.0	3.0
29	9.0	2.0	4.0	8.0	7.0	8.0	9.0	8.0	5.0	6.0
30	8.0	3.0	4.0	8.0	7.0	6.0	6.0	4.0	5.0	1.0
31	8.0	3.0	2.0	9.0	5.0	8.0	9.0	5.0	7.0	5.0
32	5.0	1.0	2.0	7.0	5.0	9.0	9.0	7.0	8.0	6.0
33	9.0	1.0	4.0	9.0	6.0	9.0	9.0	5.0	9.0	2.0
34	8.0	2.0	6.0	8.0	7.0	9.0	8.0	5.0	9.0	5.0
35	9.0	1.0	7.0	9.0	5.0	7.0	6.0	6.0	4.0	1.0
36	8.0	1.0	4.0	9.0	6.0	8.0	8.0	3.0	7.0	4.0
37	9.0	2.0	3.0	9.0	5.0	8.0	9.0	7.0	9.0	6.0
38	8.0	2.0	3.0	6.0	5.0	9.0	9.0	3.0	9.0	6.0
39	9.0	2.0	4.0	9.0	7.0	8.0	7.0	7.0	9.0	1.0
40	8.0	3.0	2.0	7.0	5.0	8.0	9.0	5.0	6.0	1.0
41	9.0	3.0	4.0	8.0	8.0	9.0	6.0	2.0	9.0	6.0
42	8.0	3.0	2.0	8.0	6.0	8.0	9.0	4.0	7.0	2.0
43	9.0	2.0	1.0	8.0	6.0	7.0	9.0	5.0	9.0	5.0
44	9.0	2.0	3.0	9.0	7.0	8.0	9.0	7.0	5.0	4.0
45	9.0	2.0	3.0	7.0	6.0	9.0	9.0	7.0	5.0	2.0
46	8.0	1.0	2.0	9.0	5.0	8.0	9.0	4.0	9.0	4.0
47	9.0	2.0	3.0	9.0	6.0	9.0	9.0	6.0	8.0	1.0
48	9.0	3.0	6.0	8.0	2.0	8.0	9.0	4.0	8.0	4.0

EXHIBIT 2 cont'd

Individual-level preference data, measured on a scale from 1 to 9, with higher numbers representing increased preference (GEOPREF.DAT).

	G20	Ford T-Bird	Audi 90	Toyota Supra	Eagle Talon	Honda Prelude	Saab 900	Pontiac Firebird	BMW 318i	Mercury Capri
49	9.0	1.0	2.0	9.0	6.0	8.0	9.0	4.0	7.0	1.0
50	9.0	3.0	6.0	9.0	6.0	9.0	8.0	8.0	7.0	5.0
51	8.0	3.0	5.0	7.0	2.0	8.0	8.0	6.0	8.0	1.0
52	9.0	5.0	4.0	7.0	1.0	2.0	5.0	1.0	9.0	3.0
53	7.0	4.0	4.0	3.0	4.0	9.0	8.0	2.0	5.0	4.0
54	7.0	2.0	6.0	5.0	3.0	7.0	6.0	4.0	8.0	6.0
55	5.0	2.0	3.0	5.0	5.0	8.0	9.0	1.0	9.0	1.0
56	4.0	5.0	6.0	5.0	4.0	9.0	8.0	4.0	6.0	4.0
57	7.0	1.0	7.0	8.0	7.0	7.0	7.0	2.0	6.0	5.0
58	5.0	3.0	3.0	7.0	2.0	8.0	7.0	2.0	9.0	6.0
59	4.0	4.0	5.0	8.0	2.0	6.0	6.0	6.0	6.0	1.0
60	8.0	4.0	9.0	4.0	5.0	5.0	5.0	2.0	7.0	4.0
61	8.0	4.0	5.0	4.0	3.0	6.0	8.0	3.0	7.0	4.0
62	7.0	5.0	7.0	7.0	6.0	6.0	6.0	5.0	7.0	3.0
63	8.0	2.0	2.0	4.0	5.0	8.0	8.0	1.0	9.0	2.0
64	5.0	6.0	4.0	7.0	4.0	4.0	5.0	1.0	8.0	1.0
65	7.0	4.0	4.0	6.0	5.0	3.0	6.0	1.0	6.0	4.0
66	8.0	2.0	9.0	3.0	5.0	7.0	8.0	4.0	6.0	2.0
67	3.0	5.0	8.0	7.0	6.0	3.0	8.0	2.0	9.0	6.0
68	6.0	1.0	3.0	5.0	2.0	9.0	7.0	2.0	6.0	5.0
69	6.0	3.0	8.0	8.0	5.0	8.0	6.0	3.0	3.0	1.0
70	7.0	2.0	8.0	8.0	3.0	9.0	7.0	4.0	4.0	5.0
71	7.0	1.0	7.0	7.0	8.0	8.0	9.0	1.0	9.0	1.0
72	6.0	5.0	5.0	5.0	4.0	6.0	9.0	4.0	8.0	2.0
73	7.0	5.0	4.0	4.0	2.0	6.0	8.0	5.0	9.0	5.0
74	8.0	5.0	6.0	6.0	6.0	7.0	7.0	4.0	8.0	4.0
75	7.0	3.0	6.0	8.0	4.0	7.0	7.0	5.0	5.0	3.0

	G20	Ford T-bird	Audi 90	Toyota Supra	Eagle Talon	Honda Prelude	Saab 900	Pontiac Firebird	BMW 318i	Mercury Capri
Base Price ($)	17,500	15,783	20,200	23,280	16,437	14,945	18,295	12,690	19,900	13,500
Length (Inches)	175	198.7	176	181.9	170.5	175.6	184.5	192.0	170.3	166.1
Width (Inches)	66.7	72.7	67.6	68.7	66.7	67.3	66.5	72.4	64.8	64.6
Height (Inches)	54.9	52.7	54.3	51.2	51.4	29.2	56.1	49.8	53.5	50.2
Curb Weight (lbs.)	2,535	3,600	3,170	3,535	3,100	2,740	2,825	3,485	2,600	2,487
Fuel Economy (Mpg) City Highway	24 32	17 24	18 24	17 22	20 25	23 27	20 26	16 24	22 27	23 28
Horspower, SAE.net (Bhp)	140@ 6,400 rpm	210@ 4,000 rpm	164@ 6,000 rpm	232@ 5,600 rpm	195@ 6,000 rpm	135@ 6,200 rpm	140@ 6,000 rpm	240@ 4,400 rpm	134@ 6,000 rpm	132@ 6,000 rpm
Warranty, Years/Miles, Bumper-to-Bumper	4/ 60,000	1/ 12,000	3/ 50,000	3/ 36,000	1/ 12,000	3/ 36,000	3/ 36,000	3/ 50,000	3/ 36,000	1/ 12,000

EXHIBIT 3
Some physical characteristics of the cars.

Segment Characteristic	Segment I (Western Yuppie, Single)	Segment II (Upwardly Mobile Families)	Segment III (American Dreamers)
Segment Size	(25%)	(45%)	(30%)
Education	College Grads	College Grads or Some College	College Grads or Some College
Predominant Employment	Professionals	White-Collar	White-Collar
Age Group	25-35	25-35	25-35
Predominant Ethnic Background	White	White	Mix (Asian, White)
Average Household Income	$81,000	$68,000	$59,000
Persons per Household	1.42	3.8	2.4
Percent Married	32%	75%	55%
Watch Late Night TV	27%	9%	17%
Watch Daytime TV	3%	45%	5%
Read Computer Magazines	39%	6%	10%
Read Business Magazines	58%	23%	27%
Read Entertainment Magazines	3%	14%	30%
Read Infant and Parenting Magazines	1%	17%	2%
Rent Movies	43%	85%	38%
Possess an American Express Card	48%	45%	75%
Own Investment Funds	24%	18%	47%
Go Fishing	2%	30%	3%
Sail, Scuba Dive or Ski	49%	2%	20%

EXHIBIT 4
Data about the sub-segments.

EXERCISES

1. Describe the two (or, if applicable, three) dimensions underlying the perceptual maps that you generated. Based on these maps, how do people in this market perceive the Infiniti G20 compared with its competitors?

2. Infiniti promoted the G20 as a Japanese car (basic version $17,500) with a German feel, basically a car that was like the BMW 318i ($20,000), but lower priced. Is this a credible claim, given the perceptions and preferences of the respondents?

3. Which attributes are most important in influencing preference for these cars in the three segments (S1, S2, and S3) shown on these maps? To which segment(s) would you market the Infiniti G20? How would you reposition the Infiniti G20 to best suit the chosen segment(s)? Briefly describe the marketing program you would use to target the chosen segment(s).

4. What ongoing research program would you recommend to Infiniti to improve its evaluation of its segmentation of the market and positioning of its G20?

5. Summarize the advantages and limitations of the software provided for this application.

POSITIONING THE ConneCtor EXERCISE

(This exercise is a follow-up to Conglomerate Inc's new PDA Case)

Background

Following the preliminary findings of their market research study, Conglomerate Inc. hired LR Inc. to help them position their new product in a specific target market segment that they tentatively called "Hard Hats." (Construction and emergency workers, primarily.)

LR Inc. reviewed the key product features that appeared to differentiate ConneCtor from its major competitors and identified the following dimensions.

Instant communication from PDA to PDA
Connectivity
Cellular phone and pager, fax and email
Calendar, scheduler, calculator and address book
Open system
Paperless note pad
Voice recognition

LR then ran two focus groups among "Hard Hats" and determined that the features that seemed to interest the groups the most were connectivity and communication. After careful discussion with Conglomerate's Ad Agency, they agreed to develop and test an ad campaign around the feature, "communication."

To test the potential effectiveness of the ad, LR recruited 75 "Hard Hats" who were given advertisements and descriptions of product features for the New PDA as well as for the following competing brands:

Sharp_5800
Sony_PIC2000
Newton_130
Hitachi
HP_200LX
Pilot_5000
Canon
Psion_3c
NEC_Pro

Respondents were then asked two sets of questions:

First, each respondent was asked to evaluate each of the brands (including the New PDA) along a 1 to 7 scale (where 1 = Worst and 7 = Best) along the following dimensions:

Good_value
Light
Reliable
Large
Ease of service
Expandability
Screen quality
Easy to use
Shows I am successful
Common brand
Economical
Permits connectivity
Permits communication
Permits effective use of spreadsheet

These data are available in a file called pdaperc.dat.

Next, each of the 75 respondents was asked to provide preference scores from 1 (like the least) to 10 (like the most) for each of the brands at their suggested retail prices. These data are available in a file called pdapref.dat.

LR was then asked to use perceptual mapping to evaluate the effectiveness of the Positioning for the New PDA.

EXERCISES

1. Describe the two (or if applicable, three) dimensions underlying the perceptual maps that you generate. Based on those maps, how do "Hard Hats" perceive ConneCtor compared with its competitors?

2. Run the analysis with the preference data. What dimensions seem to drive choice and likely market share in this market? (*Be sure to select "New PDA" when viewing the map—and remember that the right mouse button gives market share estimates.*)

3. How would you modify the ad campaign for the ConneCtor to better position it to this target segment?

4. What program of research would you recommend to refine your findings?

5. Comment on the advantages and disadvantages of the perceptual mapping approach to product positioning.

Chapter 4

TUTORIAL FOR CONJOINT ANALYSIS

Concept

Conjoint Analysis is widely employed for designing new products. It is a procedure for measuring, analyzing, and predicting customers' responses to new products and to new features of existing products. It enables companies to decompose customers' preferences for products and services (provided as descriptions or visual images) into "part-worth" utilities associated with each option of each attribute or feature of the product. They can then recombine the part worths to predict customers' preferences for any product that can be developed using the attributes and options included in the study. They can use this procedure to determine the optimal product concept or to identify market segments that value a particular product concept highly.

Software

On the **Model** menu, select **Conjoint Analysis**. You will see the following window:

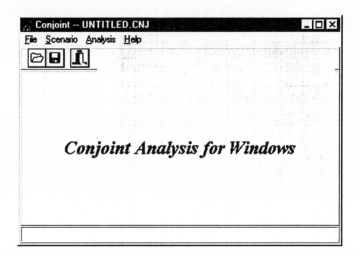

Using the **File** menu you can **Open** an existing conjoint analysis file (if you have one). For the Forte Hotel Design exercise, open file hotel.cnj. Otherwise, proceed to the **Scenario** menu. You can also **Save** information from a session to a file and retrieve it later.

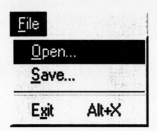

The tutorial consists of three sections: (1) Designing a conjoint study, (2) Obtaining data about customer preferences, and (3) Conducting market simulations. For the Forte Hotel Design exercise, we have already completed the design and data collection stages.

Designing a conjoint study

The first step in designing a conjoint study is to generate a scenario by specifying the product attributes and their possible options. To do this you perform three substeps.

1. Identify the major attributes of the product category of interest. For example, "Leisure activities available to patrons" could be a major attribute in designing a new hotel.

   ■ Identify attributes by asking experts, surveying consumers or conducting focus groups. Attributes can be structural characteristics, product features or options, appearance of product, or even marketing-mix variables, such as price.
   ■ Omit from the analysis attributes on which all products and new product concepts are similar. For example, if all hotels offer express check-out and that service is considered essential in all new hotels, you can omit it from the study. It is also important to use attributes that customers in the target segment care about.

   On the **Scenario** menu, select **Edit Attributes and Levels**:

   You will see the following screen:

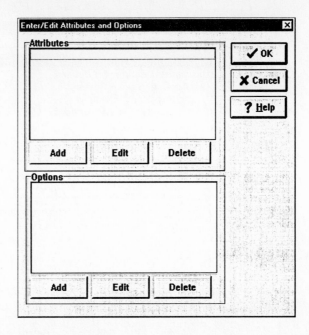

Click the **Add** button under **Attributes** to specify the product or service attributes of interest in the study. You can add up to six attributes. You can edit a previously entered attribute by clicking **Edit**. You can also **Delete** any attribute entered.

NOTE: *The program uses only the first 10 characters of the names you provide.*

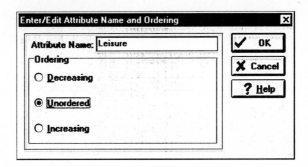

You can use the **Ordering** option to specify whether preferences will be decreasing, unordered, or increasing with respect to levels of this attribute. This educational version permits only the unordered option.

2. Once you have entered your list of attributes, you must enter at least two options of each attribute that are available, as shown in the example below for the attribute Leisure. Use the **Add** button to list levels. You should choose the major options already available in the market, as well as new options being considered for the proposed new product. Use the arrow keys or the mouse to select the attributes for which you want to **Add** the appropriate levels.

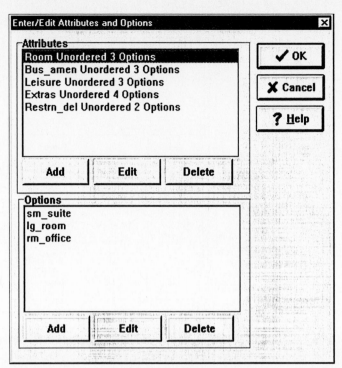

3. To generate a set of products for customer evaluation, describe each product as a combination of attribute options. After you have entered all the attributes and attribute options, click **OK**. You will see the following screen:

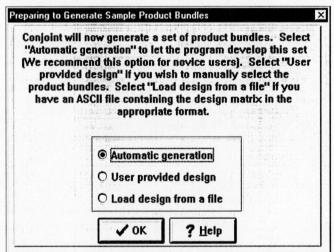

Automatic generation produces a set of orthogonal product profiles. Unless you are experienced in conjoint analysis, select **Automatic Generation** (the default option). If you select this option, the program generates a subset of products from the total set of products containing all possible combinations of attribute options. The selected subset is such that it ensures that every option of every attribute is present in a sufficient number of products to allow for the proper estimation of the importance of that attribute option to a consumer.

Knowledgeable users can select their own subsets of products using criteria other than orthogonality. You can specify a set of product profiles for analysis by choosing **User-Provided Design**. The program will then display a list of packages that it selected automatically. You can use this list as a starting point for designing your own set of packages.

NOTE: *Clicking OK here brings you back to the initial screen.*

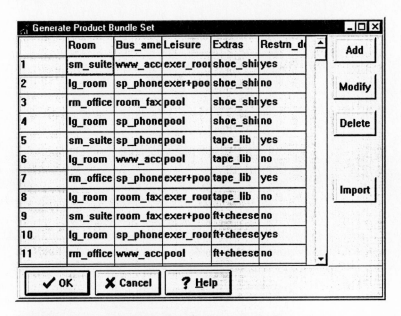

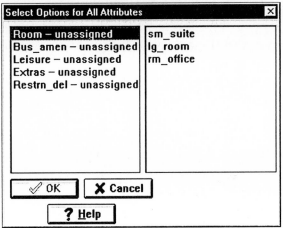

You can also choose **Load Design from File** to load your own design matrix from an external ASCII text file. An example file for a five-attribute design matrix is shown below:

```
0 0 0 0 0
1 1 2 0 1
2 2 1 0 0
1 1 1 0 1
0 1 1 1 0
1 0 1 1 1
2 1 2 1 0
1 2 0 1 1
0 2 2 2 1
1 1 0 2 0
2 0 1 2 1
1 1 1 2 0
0 1 1 3 1
1 2 1 3 0
2 1 0 3 1
1 0 2 3 0
```

In specifying a design matrix, follow the convention for labeling attribute options shown in the example above: Attribute 1 (the first column) has three options labeled 0, 1, and 2; Attribute 5 has two options labeled 0 and 1.

For this tutorial, we have already specified a design matrix, completing section 1. For the rest of this tutorial, we will use this predefined example. If you have not already done so, go to the **File** menu and click **Open** to load the hotel.cnj file.

Assessing preferences of customers

In this section, we demonstrate how to obtain respondent evaluations for the selected products. For purposes of illustration, you will be the respondent.

Begin the utility assessment procedure by opening the **Scenario** menu and choosing **Utility Assessment**.

You will see a dialog box requesting an ID under which your preferences will be stored for further analysis. Enter your name or a unique ID and click **OK**.

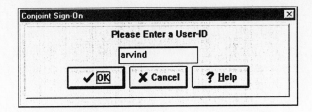

You will see the following screen:

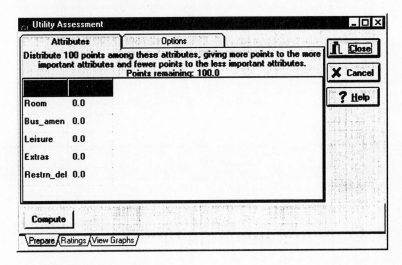

Under **Utility Assessment**, you can select either **Prepare** or **Ratings** procedures or do both in sequence.

1. ***Prepare*** *(also known as self-explicated ratings)*: To complete the "Prepare" task, you must provide information regarding (1) your relative preferences for the attributes, and (2) relative preferences for the available options of each attribute. You have 100 points to distribute across the attributes.

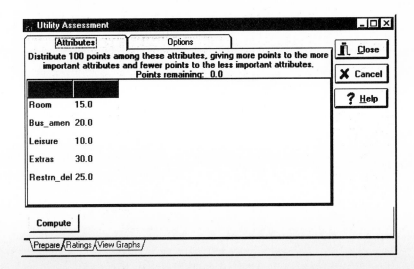

After you assess the importance, or weight, of each attribute, click the **Options** tab and rank the options of the Leisure attribute. Click the **Next Attrib** button to go to the next attribute, which in this case, is "Extras." After you enter your rankings for all options of all attributes, click **Compute**.

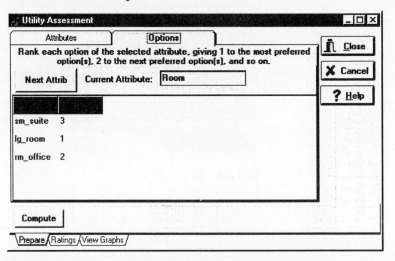

2. ***Ratings option***: Choose the ratings task by clicking the **Ratings** tab at the bottom of the screen. You will see the dialog box below:

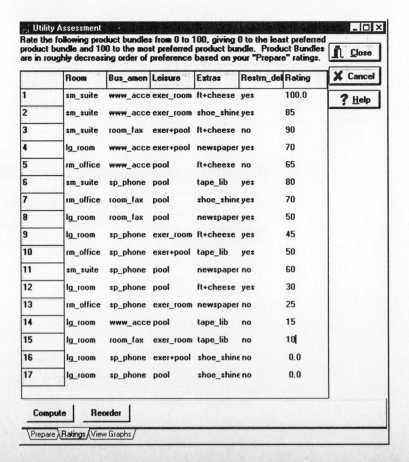

In the "Rating" column, enter a value between 0 and 100 to re-flect your preference for each of the hotel packages presented, one per row. If you complete the prepare task before selecting the ratings task, the program will already have sequenced the packages accord-ing to your Prepare ratings. The most-preferred package appears at the top with a value of 100, and the least-preferred package appears at the bottom with a value of 0. Interspersed between these two packages are a carefully selected set of alternative packages for you to evaluate. If you initiated the ratings task without completing the Prepare task, the program will list the packages in random order. Doing the Prepare task before the Ratings task makes the ratings task easier.

At any time during the ratings task, you can click **Reorder** to order the packages from most preferred to least preferred, which makes the ratings process easier:

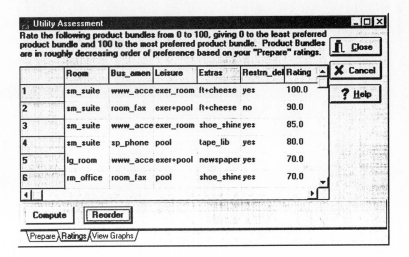

Once you have rated all the packages, click **Compute**. The pro-gram then computes the utility function corresponding to the values you provided in the "Ratings" column.

3. ***Graphics option***: Once you have finished the ratings task, click **View Graphs** to see a graphical depiction of the utility function generated using your ratings. For consistency the utility function is scaled to lie between 0 and 100 as it does in the prepare task.

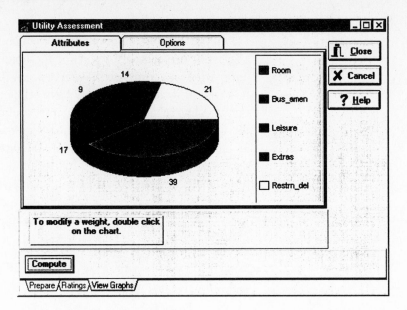

By clicking the **Options** tab, you can see a bar graph of the part-worth utilities corresponding to each option of each attribute, as shown below.

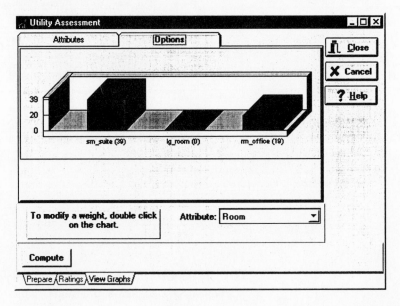

After viewing the graphs, you may think that the relative weights for attributes and attribute options shown in the graphs do not convey your true preferences. In this case, you can alter the weights assigned to any attribute or attribute option. Double-click on either the pie chart (to change part worths of attributes) or the bar graph (to change part worths of attribute options).

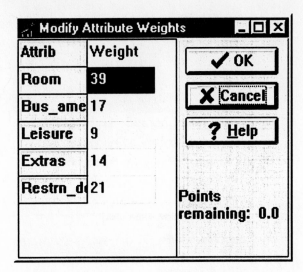

NOTE: *For consistency, attribute weights must sum to 100, and weights for attribute options must range from 0 to a maximum value corresponding to the weight given to that attribute.*

You can go back and forth between **Prepare**, **Ratings**, and **Graphs** as many times as necessary, until you are sure that the utility function shown in the graphs reflects your true preferences. When you finish this task, the program will save a copy of the final utility function under a file name that includes the ID you used to sign on. Click **Close**.

Conducting market simulations

Once you have obtained utility functions from a sample of respondents, the fun part begins. Using the program you can design new products that will be attractive to the target segment in the presence of existing products in the marketplace. The success of new products depends on how well their attribute options match customer preferences compared to the competitive offerings in the market. Go to the **Analysis** menu. You must perform the following tasks before you can evaluate new product concepts:

1. From the **Analysis** menu, choose **Load Part Worth File(s).** Select any subset of respondents for analysis using any suitable criteria. For example, you can select only male respondents for further analysis. You can then repeat the analyses for other subsegments. The program stores utility functions under the ID name of each respondent who provided the data, adding the extension .PRT to the ID name.

   NOTE: *Once you have saved part-worth data in a file, you don't have to reload these files each time you run the program. For the Forte Hotel exercise, the hotel.cnj file includes the part-worth files of all 40 respondents. When you do the exercise, you can go directly to*

Create/Edit Existing Product Profiles or to other commands on the Analysis menu.

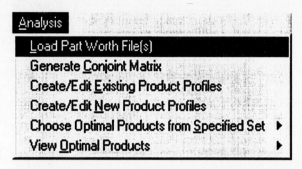

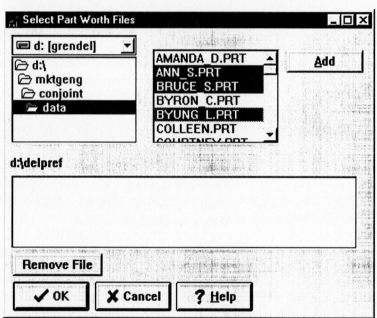

Select all the files you want to include and click **Add**. (To select multiple files at the same time, press the Ctrl key while clicking the file name). For our analysis, we will select all 40 respondents. After selecting the files, click **OK**.

2. Next load these files into the program by selecting **Generate Conjoint Matrix**, as shown below. Use the scroll bar to view sections of the matrix that are hidden from view.

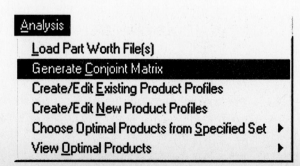

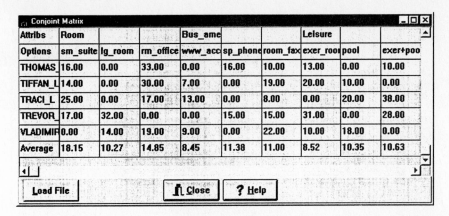

The last row of the conjoint matrix shows the average part worth of each attribute option across the selected respondents. The average part worth gives a good indication of the attribute options that are attractive to the selected group of customers. After viewing this, click **Close**.

You can also directly load an ASCII file containing the part-worth data of a number of respondents by clicking on the **Load File** button and specifying the file name. The file to be loaded should have the format described under "Load an ASCII file containing the data in the appropriate format" described in the **Introduction to Software** section of this volume. Note that if you load a new file, any previously loaded data will be removed before the new data is entered into the data matrix.

3. To specify a set of existing products against which proposed new concepts will compete, go to the **Analysis** menu and select the **Create/Edit Existing Product Profiles**.

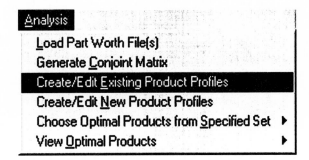

You will see the following screen:

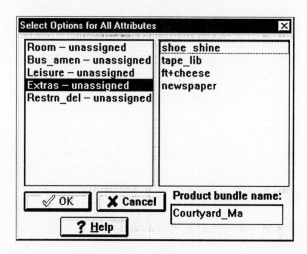

When you click **Add** or **Modify**, you will see the following screen:

Specify each product by selecting the appropriate attribute options corresponding to that product. It is advisable to include only products that are likely to compete directly with the proposed new product concepts.

If more than one existing product has the same set of attribute options, you should define just one of them. Once you have defined a product, the screen will look as shown. You can also provide a unique name associated with this product. Here, we called this package the "Courtyard by Marriott."

After you define all existing products of interest for this analysis, click **OK**. You will see a screen similar to the following:

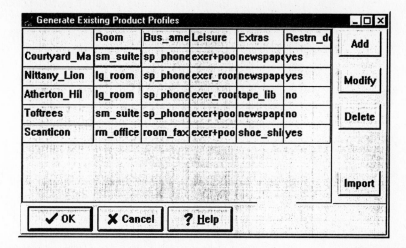

4. Next specify a set of candidate new product-concepts. (If you do not specify any new-product profiles for analysis, you can compute the estimated market shares of the existing products. This serves as a validity check of the data set.) From the **Analysis** menu, choose **Create/Edit New Product Profiles** as shown below.

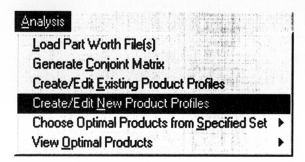

Specify the attribute options for the new product using the procedure we described earlier for creating existing product profiles.

5. By now, you have specified most of the information that Conjoint Analysis needs to simulate the market performance of the selected products. From the **Analysis** menu, click **Choose Optimal Products from Specified Set**. You will be offered three choice rules for assessing the market performance of the new products:

> ***Maximum utility rule***: Each respondent is assumed to select the product that provides the highest utility among the competing products and a specific new product concept being evaluated. Conjoint Analysis evaluates each new product concept in turn in competition with the existing products. The maximum utility rule is the preferred analysis option if customers buy products in the product category infrequently.

Share of utility rule: Each respondent's share of purchases of a particular product is considered to be a function of the utility for that product as compared to the total utility for all products in the competitive set. This analysis option is most suitable for products customers buy frequently.

Logit choice rule: The share for each product for each respondent is considered to be a function of the "weighted" utility for that product as compared to the total weighed utility for all products in the competitive set. The weighting is done using an exponential function. This analysis option is an alternative to the share-of-utility model for frequently purchased products.

The market-share predictions made by both the share-of-utility and logit choice rules are sensitive to the scale range on which utility is measured. The market share prediction of the share-of-utility rule will change if you add a constant value to the computed utility of each product, but it is not altered if you multiply all utility values by a constant. On the other hand, market-share predictions of the logit choice rule are not altered if you add a constant to the utilities, but they are altered if you multiply all utilities by a constant.

In computing market shares, we follow Green and Krieger (1985) who first normalized the utility scale for each respondent such that the least preferred option of each attribute has a utility equal to 0, and the utility scale has a range from 0 to K, where K is the number of attributes.

It is best not to interpret the market-share prediction for a new product in an absolute sense. Instead, view the share in a relative sense—those new products that have higher predicted market shares are likely to perform better in the market than those that have lower predicted shares.

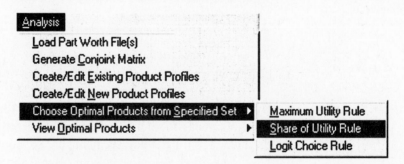

6. After you choose an analysis option, you will see a pie graph showing the market share for the first new-product concept. The following screen shows that the market share for the new-product concept called "Profesnl_1" is 16.44 percent when it is introduced into the market with four existing competitors. Click **Next** to see the graph for the next concept.

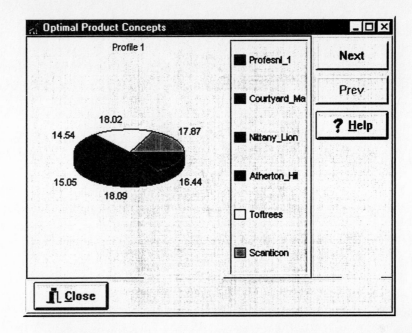

7. You can also do a complete search of all possible product profiles by going to the **Analysis** menu and choosing **View Optimal Products**. If you choose this command the program will select the top four performing product profiles according to the choice rule that you specify.

NOTE: *Products that you have defined in the existing product profiles are excluded from this evaluation.*

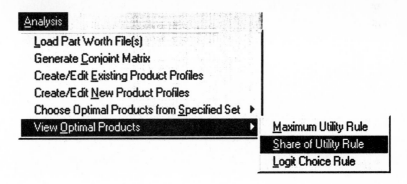

Limitations of the educational version of the software:

Maximum number of attributes:	6
Maximum number of levels per attribute:	4
Maximum number of existing product profiles:	8
Maximum number of new product concepts that can be evaluated:	5,000

References

Green, Paul E. and Wind, Yoram 1975, "New Way to Measure Consumers' Judgments," *Harvard Business Review*, Vol. 53, No. 4 (July-August), pp. 107-117.

Lilien, Gary L. and Rangaswamy, Arvind 1998, *Marketing Engineering: Computer-Assisted Marketing Analysis and Planning*, Chapter 7, Addison Wesley Longman, Reading, Massachusetts.

Wind, Jerry; Green, Paul E.; Shifflet, Douglas; and Scarbrough, Marsha 1989, "The Courtyard by Marriott: Designing a Hotel Facility with Consumer-based Marketing Models," *Interfaces*, Vol. 19, No. 1 (January-February), pp. 25-47.

FORTE HOTEL DESIGN CASE[*]

Forte Executive Innes

Forte Hotels, a large European hotel chain, is developing a new hotel chain in the United States. The chain, named Forte Executive Innes, will combine the ambiance of a European hotel with American functionality and convenience. Forte decided to invest in this hotel chain partly to take advantage of the increasing numbers of business people traveling from Europe to the United States.

Company background

Forte Hotels is the United Kingdom's largest hotel chain. Its hotel brands include Le Meridien, Forte Crest, Forte Posthouse, Forte Agip, and Forte Travelodge. In addition Forte Hotels includes an international group of 80 upscale hotels such as the Watergate Hotel, Washington, D.C., Hyde Park Hotel, London, and King Edward Hotel, Toronto. Recently the company's chairman, Sir Rocco Forte, announced that he plans to sell the Travelodge chain in the United States. In its place Forte Hotels will develop a new chain targeted toward European and American business travelers, Forte Executive Inne.

Forte's strategy in developing the new chain is twofold. European business travelers in the United States will recognize the Forte name and associate it with comfort and service. Forte executives also expect that American business travelers will associate the new chain with "pampering" that is often lacking in the mid-priced hotel chains, while at the same time perceiving the hotel to have all the functionality of American hotel chains. Although the hotels will have a European ambiance, the facilities and services will be comparable to those available in such hotel chains as Hilton, Sheraton, and Courtyard by Marriott.

Preliminary evaluation

A recent survey indicated that the top three reasons business travelers choose a hotel are price, location, and brand name. Forte Executive Innes would be mid-priced, around $100 per night. The company is in the process of securing several prime locations near suburban commercial centers throughout the United States. In addition, the company will leverage the Forte brand name in naming the new chain. Forte now faces the challenge of fine-tuning the specific characteristics of the hotel to

---

[*] This case describes a hypothetical situation. It was developed by Bruce Semisch under the guidance of Professor Arvind Rangaswamy.

insure that it will appeal to both American and European business travelers.

A search of business databases provided some preliminary insights on the preferences of business travelers. Among men (60 percent of business travelers in the United States), price, location, and convenience are among the top reasons why a business traveler might try a new hotel. Women travelers place more emphasis on safety and cleanliness than do men. Although these considerations, combined with the overall image of the brand name, are important in generating trial, it is the hotel's unique characteristics (attributes) that encourage repeat visits. Other recent surveys have suggested a range of potential amenities that interest at least 30 percent of business travelers. These include in-room computer facilities; on-site conference facilities; rooms with well-lit work areas with large desks and swivel chairs; and telecommunication facilities, such as speaker phones and data-ports. A survey by a leading credit card company suggests that about half the European business travelers to the United States look for hotels that will look after them and let them relax. The others tended to look for hotels that would let them finish their business assignments quickly and efficiently. Given these preliminary insights, Forte realized that it needed to thoroughly understand the preferences of the hotel's target market to create a successful new hotel chain.

Conjoint Analysis (Matching hotel attributes to customer preferences)

As a first step, the company decided to explore consumer preferences for five key attributes on which Forte Executive Innes could be differentiated: room type, business amenities, leisure facilities, conveniences and extras, and restaurants and dining. Within each attribute, it defined several different options (Exhibit 1). It did not include hotel features that are common to all existing and proposed hotels among the options. Thus for comparison purposes, it considered hotel room types of roughly the same square-foot area, with data-ports and other facilities in the rooms and front-desk faxing services.

Forte's challenge was to decide which combination of the attribute options in Exhibit 1 would most appeal to its target audience. The management team has authorized you to use conjoint analysis to determine this in a "scientific manner." It has recruited 300 business travelers to participate in the conjoint analysis study. For this exercise, you will use the information obtained from 40 of the respondents (Exhibit 2).

EXERCISES

1. **Design**: On the **Scenario** menu of the Conjoint Analysis program, choose **Edit Attributes and Levels** to explore the design of this

conjoint study (section 1 of the tutorial). Briefly summarize the advantages and limitations of describing products as bundles of attribute options.

2. ***Utility assessment***: Use the **Utility Assessment** command to explore your own trade-offs for the various attributes and options Forte Inne is considering (section 2 of the tutorial). First complete the prepare task (self-explicated ratings), and then complete the ratings task. Each member of a project group should do a separate utility assessment. When you are finished, note down the final set of weights for each attribute and attribute option.

   Based on your experiences in completing these tasks, summarize the advantages and limitations of conjoint analysis for obtaining preference data from customers.

3. ***Analysis***: Use the **Analysis** menu (section 3 of the tutorial) to assess the viability of the four specific hotel concepts (Profesnl_1, Profesnl_2, Tourist, and Deluxe) that Forte is exploring for the State College area. Base this evaluation on the preferences of a sample of 40 business travelers given in the case and the rough cost estimates summarized in Exhibit 3. The preference data is already included in the hotel.cnj file. The base cost to build each hotel room (without the attributes and options listed in Exhibit 3) is expected to be about $40,000 for a 150 to 200-room hotel, regardless of the mix of room types.

   Identify the optimal product concept from among those Forte is considering. Explain how you arrived at your recommendation.

4. Would you recommend product concepts other than the four Forte is considering for the State College market? Explain how you arrived at your recommendation(s).

5. Summarize the major advantages and limitations of a conjoint study for new-product design. What conditions favor the use of this approach in the hotel industry? (Consider such factors as types of customers and market conditions in responding to this question).

6. After hearing about the study, a manager at Forte claimed that "A conjoint study is a major deterrent to excellence in hotel design. It's a crutch for managers with no vision and conviction. On the surface, it sounds sensible enough: Find out exactly what features customers prefer before you finalize the design. But in practice, this is impossible. Customers cannot tell you what they really prefer without experiencing all the choices available to them. Even if you show them pictures or prototypes, the preferences they express are apt to veer off in the direction of mediocrity. This type of study gives you a Hyundai with a Mercedes grille, Prince tennis rackets endorsed by Ed McMahon, Big Macs with everything, and hotels with no per-

sonality! You would not produce a Mazda Miata, a Hermes tie, or the movie "Jurassic Park" with this technique." Do you agree with this statement? Why or why not?

Reference

Green, Paul E. and Krieger, Abba M. 1986, "Choice Rules and Sensitivity Analysis in Conjoint Simulators," Working Paper, The Wharton School, University of Pennsylvania.

Attribute [Abbreviation]	Possible Options [Abbreviation]

Room type (All same size) [Room]	• Small suite [sm_suite]
	  A small suite with a small bedroom area and a separate sitting area with a couch, TV, and coffee table.
	• Large standard room [lg_room]
	  A room about three feet longer than a standard room with two queen-sized beds.
	• Room with large desk and swivel chair [rm_office]
	  A room of the same dimensions as the large standard room with only one queen-sized bed and a well-lit work area with a large desk and swivel chair in place of the other bed.

Business Amenities [Bus_amen]	• World Wide Web (WWW) access [www_access]
	  A computer complete with software (e.g. Netscape) with access to Internet and the WWW, at a low hourly connection rate ($2 to $3 per hour).
	• Speakerphone in room [sp_phone]
	  A speakerphone for group business discussions.
	• In-room fax machine [room_fax]
	  A fax machine and a private fax number that expires at checkout.

Leisure Facilities [Leisure]	• Exercise room [exerc_room]:
	  A room equipped with Nautilus machines, free weights, stationary bikes, tread mills, stair climbing machines, and a sauna, that is open 24 hours a day.
	• Pool [pool]:
	  A standard rectangular indoor lap pool with shallow and deep ends.
	• Small exercise room and small pool [exerc+pool]:
	  An exercise room that lacks some of the features described above (e.g. no sauna, and fewer machines) and a round pool for recreational swimming, not a lap pool.

Conveniences & Extras [Extras]	• Complimentary shoe shine [shoe_shine]
	  Shoes left at the front desk or outside the room at night are shined and returned by a specified time in the morning.
	• Videotape library [tape_lib]
	  A large selection of tapes will be listed in a catalog in the room and available through room service.
	• Complimentary fruit and cheese bowl. [ft+cheese]
	  A complimentary fruit and gourmet cheese bowl in the room.
	• Free newspaper. [newspaper]
	  A complimentary copy of *USA Today* outside the door.

Restaurant Delivery [Restrn_del]	• Yes [yes]
	  From a book of menus from nearby restaurants, patrons can order food through room service, and a hotel employee will pick up and deliver the food.
	• No [no]
	  No restaurant delivery service available.

EXHIBIT 1
Attributes and Options

	Room	Bus. Amen.	Lei-sure	Ex-tras	Restrn Delivery	Sm Suite	Lg Room	Rm Office	WWW Access	Sp phone	Room Fax	Exer-cise Room	Pool	Exer. + Pool	Shoe Shine	Tape Lib.	Ft+ Che-ese	News-paper	Del. Yes	Del. No
1	47	21	16	11	5	47	0	20	21	0	10	12	16	0	10	0	8	11	5	0
2	23	29	7	18	23	23	0	7	0	15	29	7	0	5	9	5	18	0	0	23
3	15	38	9	21	17	15	0	12	0	14	38	4	0	9	5	7	0	21	0	17
4	20	27	10	20	23	20	0	16	10	0	27	8	10	0	0	12	20	16	23	0
5	21	26	21	21	11	21	10	0	12	26	0	0	21	3	21	9	13	0	0	11
6	22	25	12	22	19	8	0	22	13	25	0	0	12	6	22	11	0	15	0	19
7	33	16	13	33	5	16	0	33	0	16	10	13	0	10	0	11	33	18	0	5
8	24	23	14	24	15	13	0	24	10	23	0	14	0	4	8	0	24	12	15	0
9	34	22	6	22	16	0	12	34	9	22	0	0	5	6	15	0	22	8	16	0
10	26	21	16	19	18	26	0	10	21	0	14	9	16	0	0	14	7	19	18	0
11	11	52	10	17	10	0	9	11	52	13	0	0	8	10	17	6	13	0	0	10
12	19	22	18	24	17	0	14	19	9	0	22	10	18	0	24	5	0	7	17	0
13	28	37	19	12	4	12	0	28	5	0	37	0	19	11	8	12	0	6	4	0
14	30	19	20	13	18	14	0	30	7	0	19	20	10	0	4	6	0	13	0	18
15	47	25	9	12	7	0	7	47	0	8	25	9	6	0	4	12	8	0	0	7
16	34	23	12	14	17	34	0	11	23	13	0	4	12	0	5	0	8	14	17	0
17	27	42	7	8	16	27	0	23	0	13	42	0	4	7	8	6	0	3	0	16
18	34	16	16	21	13	34	0	30	0	16	11	0	16	11	21	0	14	8	13	0
19	50	19	11	8	12	50	27	0		0	19	4	11	0	7	0	8	5	4	12
20	34	27	14	10	15	34	0	16	6	27	0	8	0	14	4	0	10	8	0	15
21	33	29	3	26	9	28	0	33	11	29	0	0	1	3	6	0	26	4	0	9
22	22	22	12	24	20	0	16	22	5	0	22	12	6	0	24	8	0	12	0	20
23	31	10	10	18	31	8	0	31	8	0	10	10	4	0	0	7	15	18	31	0
24	20	21	9	41	9	20	0	14	0	7	21	9	0	5	41	13	10	0	0	9
25	31	14	25	18	12	14	31	0	14	0	13	7	25	0	13	0	18	8	12	0
26	29	11	31	16	13	10	0	29	7	11	0	0	31	17	2	9	16	0	13	0
27	18	27	27	14	14	0	7	18	0	27	18	12	0	27	4	9	0	14	0	14
28	27	4	56	10	3	0	27	7	4	0	2	56	19	0	4	10	0	6	3	0
29	16	29	29	12	14	0	16	8	16	29	0	0	29	20	0	12	6	9	14	0
30	45	2	32	2	19	45	0	17	0	2	0	0	15	32	2	0	0	1	0	19
31	16	16	33	13	22	6	16	0	0	16	9	7	0	33	5	0	9	13	0	22
32	19	22	32	11	16	0	19	5	10	22	0	32	16	0	9	11	0	3	16	0
33	43	12	25	8	12	13	43	0	11	0	12	10	25	0	0	8	6	4	0	12
34	37	9	39	3	12	10	37	0	0	9	3	0	39	21	3	0	3	0	12	0
35	17	24	32	15	12	17	7	0	7	24	0	5	0	32	2	15	8	0	0	12
36	72	7	10	5	6	72	43	0	7	6	0	7	0	10	0	0	5	5	0	6
37	36	18	24	8	14	36	18	0	18	8	0	0	11	24	0	6	8	8	14	0
38	25	13	38	12	12	25	0	17	13	0	8	0	20	38	0	10	4	12	0	12
39	20	19	32	18	11	11	20	0	9	0	19	14	0	32	4	0	18	12	11	0
40	32	15	31	12	10	17	32	0	0	15	15	31	0	28	12	7	0	5	10	0

EXHIBIT 2
Preference Data for 40 respondents

	Incremental fixed costs per room ($) at the time of construction	Average expected incremental contribution per day per room ($)
WWW access	2,500	3.00
Speaker phone in room	200	2.00
In-room fax machine	600	2.50
Exercise room	1,500	-2.00
Pool	3,000	-4.00
Small exercise room & small pool	3,500	-4.50
Complimentary shoe shine	30	-0.50
Videotape library	300	-0.50
Complimentary fruit & cheese bowl	100	-5.00
Newspaper	-	-1.00
Restaurant delivery	100	-3.00
No restaurant delivery	-	-

EXHIBIT 3
Cost Data

Chapter 5

TUTORIAL FOR THE ASSESSOR PRETEST MARKET MODEL (ASSESSOR)

Concept

Pretest market forecasting and analysis occur after the product and packaging are available (at least in trial quantities), advertising copy is ready, and the firm has formulated a preliminary plan for the marketing-mix elements such as the price, channels of distribution, and the market budget. Given these inputs ASSESSOR is intended to

1. Predict the new product's long-term market share and sales volume over time
2. Estimate the sources of the new product's share—that is, whether it draws its market share from competitors' brands or from other products of the same firm ("cannibalization")
3. Generate diagnostic information to improve the product, the advertising copy, and other launch materials
4. Permit rough evaluation of alternative marketing plans, including different prices, package designs, and the like

Exhibits 1 and 2 summarize the overall structure of the model and the measurement approach for calibrating the model. ASSESSOR consists of two models: a preference model and a trial-repeat model. If these two models provide similar forecasts, it strengthens our confidence in the forecasts. If they provide very different forecasts, an analysis of the sources of discrepancies should provide us with useful diagnostic information.

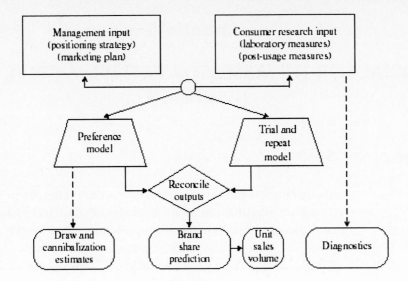

EXHIBIT 1

Overview of ASSESSOR modeling sequence. The model uses managerial judgment and consumer research data to make sales forecasts (brand share and sales volume) and offer diagnostics (e.g., draw and cannibalization estimates and reasons for purchase of new product). *Source:* Silk and Urban 1978, and Urban and Katz 1983.

Design	Procedure	Measurement
O_1	Respondent screening and recruitment (personal interview)	Criteria for target-group identification (e.g., product-class usage) Criteria
O_2	Premeasurement for established brands (self-administered questionnaire)	Composition of "relevant set" of established brands, attribute weights and ratings, and preferences.
X_1	Exposure to advertising for established brands and new brand	
$[O_3]$	Measurement of reactions to the advertising materials (self-administered questionnaire)	Optional, e.g., likability and believability ratings of advertising materials
X_2	Simulated shopping trip and exposure to display of new and established brands	
O_4	Purchase opportunity (choice recorded by research personnel)	Brand(s) purchased
X_3	Home use, or consumption of new brand	
O_5	Post-usage measurement (telephone interview)	New-brand usage rate, satisfaction ratings, and repeat-purchase propensity; attribute ratings and preferences for "relevant set" of established brands plus the new brand

EXHIBIT 2

Overview of ASSESSOR data-collection procedure. *Source:* Silk and Urban 1978, p. 174, Table 1.

Our ASSESSOR Excel spreadsheet incorporates both the trial and repeat model and the preference model. Both models are essentially self-contained and they complement each other. The ASSESSOR Excel spreadsheet is designed to accompany the Harvard Business School case, "Johnson Wax: Enhance (A)," which gives more detailed explanations of these models.

Part 1—Trial and repeat model

On the **Model** menu, select **Pretest Market Model** (assessor.xls) to get to the introductory screen. Select the **Trial & Repeat Model** and click on the **Next** button.

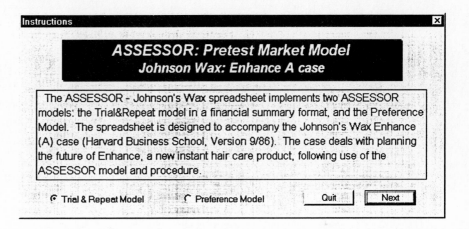

You need to run the Trial & Repeat Model before running the Preference Model. In this implementation, the Trial & Repeat Model generates one of the inputs to the Preference Model (Net Cumulative Trial from Ad).

You will see the input box for the Trial & Repeat Model. Click **Response Mode** to assign parameter values indirectly or click **Manual Mode** to do it directly.

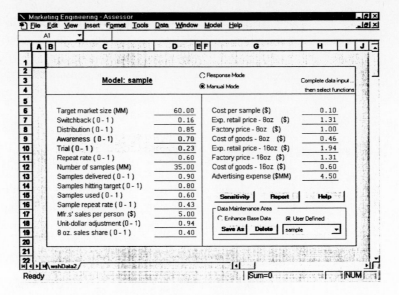

Note that no **Set Up** button is available in the **Manual Mode**.

The response mode allows you to define functional relationships between advertising expenditures and awareness and between advertising expenditures and the trial rate. Variations in the advertising level are reflected in costs and in revenues. In contrast the manual mode represents the simple "dumb spreadsheet" approach, where sales are independent of advertising.

Clicking the **Set Up** button while in the **Response Mode** brings you to the following box.

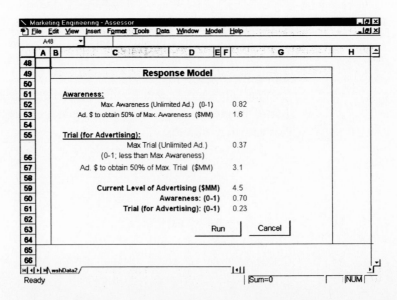

You must provide parameter values to calibrate two simple response curves that represent the effect of advertising expenditure on awareness and trial. The modified exponential function underlies these two response curves. When you are finished, click **Run** to get back to the model input screen.

Once you have provided the necessary inputs for the Trial & Repeat model, save the work. Click **Save As** to save your input data and to assign a name to the data set. Any saved data set can be accessed later by selecting **User Defined** and then selecting the data set from the pull-down menu directly underneath. Click **Delete** to remove data cases.

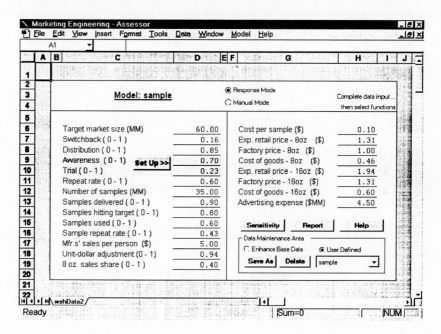

There are two ways to view the results of the Trial & Repeat model: (1) **Sensitivity** and (2) **Report**.

Sensitivity analysis: Selecting **Sensitivity** opens a new dialog sheet that lets you see the effects on Market Share and Return on Sales of changing one of the input parameters. In this box, we have opted to investigate the impact of advertising expense.

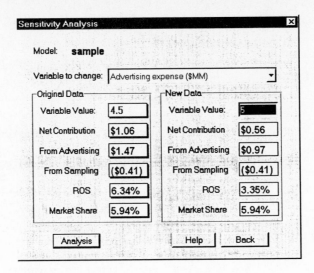

NOTE: *The effects of changing the amount of advertising expense will differ depending on whether the values for Trial and Awareness in the active input data set are based on the Manual Mode or the Response Mode.*

Click **Back** to go back to the model input screen.

Report: Click **Report** to see two pages of output from the Trial & Repeat Model. It shows the effects of advertising and sampling on market share, along with some financial results.

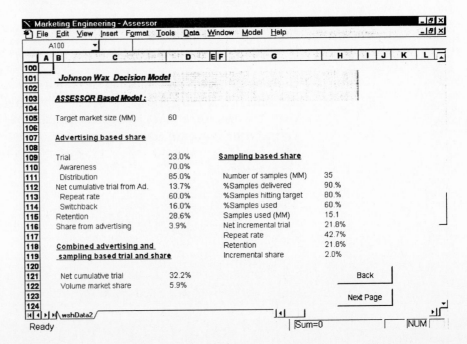

Part 2—Preference model

To switch to the Preference Model, you must go back to the introductory dialog box from the **Model** menu, choose **Introduction**.
Click **Preference Model** and **Next**.

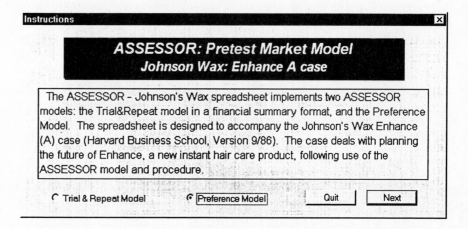

The Preference Model **Main Menu** lists the functions of the model.

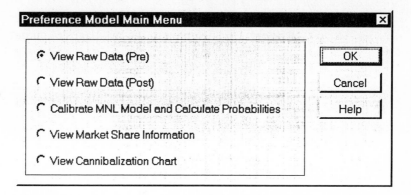

NOTE*: You can access the Preference Model* **Main Menu** *under the* **Model** *menu in the menu bar (you cannot access it while working in the Trial & Repeat Model).*

Step 1

First you can view the input data for the respondents prior to their exposure to advertising and to simulated shopping (preusage) and after exposure (postusage). The preusage data sheet shows scaled preference ratings from each respondent for each brand in the test and the brand last purchased prior to advertising exposure and the simulated shopping experience. On the **Model** menu, choose **Main Menu**, and click **View Raw Data (Post)** to see the postusage data sheet. It contains scaled preference ratings from the survey conducted after the respondents have had an opportunity to use the product. The pre- and the post-data sets include information only from respondents who responded to both surveys.

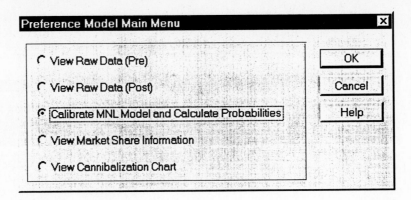

Step 2

Central to the Preference Model is the third option, **Calibrate MNL (Multinomial Logit) Model and Calculate Probabilities**. Click this option to start the estimation of the MNL coefficient (b) and the calculation of the market share estimates based on this estimated coefficient.

First you need to enter the number of brands and the number of respondents. These parameters are dependent on the ASSESSOR test data. For the Johnson Wax: Enhance case, we have already entered this information.

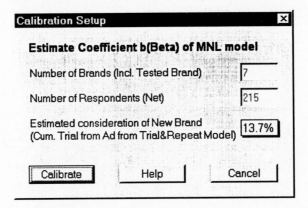

The Trial & Repeat model calculates a value for "cumulative trial from advertising," which serves as a proxy for the likely purchase of Enhance by respondents who are not subjected to the simulated shopping experience. Click **Calibrate** to start the estimation procedure and then **OK**. The program will then display the computed b coefficient. Click **OK** to continue.

The program computes the b coefficient of the MNL model using the Solver tool. It will also compute the choice probabilities of each brand for each respondent, and it will convert these probabilities into market shares using the estimated (b) coefficient. While the macro is running, the status bar will inform you about its progress.

NOTE: *By choosing* **View Raw Data (Pre)** *and* **View Raw Data (Post)** *you can access the probability estimates (see also Step 4).*

Step 3

After the program calibrates the MNL model and estimates the probabilities, select **View Market Share Information** to see information on market shares and draw estimates, as shown below:

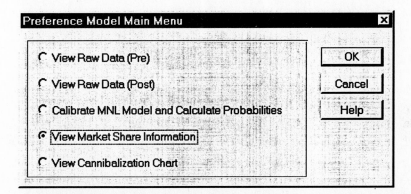

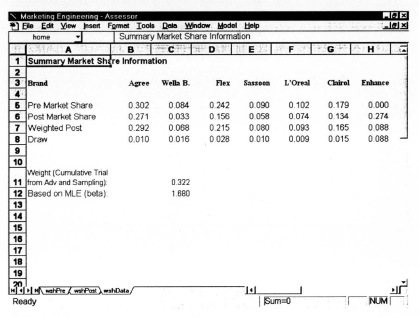

Brand	Agree	Wella B.	Flex	Sassoon	L'Oreal	Clairol	Enhance
Pre Market Share	0.302	0.084	0.242	0.090	0.102	0.179	0.000
Post Market Share	0.271	0.033	0.156	0.058	0.074	0.134	0.274
Weighted Post	0.292	0.068	0.215	0.080	0.093	0.165	0.088
Draw	0.010	0.016	0.028	0.010	0.009	0.015	0.088
Weight (Cumulative Trial from Adv and Sampling):		0.322					
Based on MLE (beta):		1.680					

You can also select **View Cannibalization Chart** to see the chart titled **Market Share Draw** which shows the estimated impact of cannibalization.

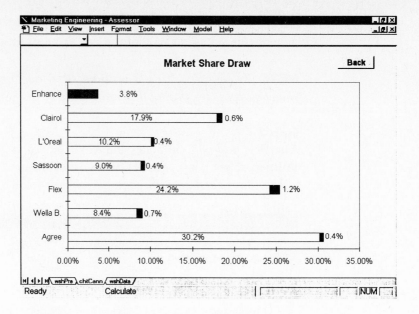

Step 4

If you want to investigate the output of the Preference Model in more detail, you can look at the estimated probabilities (which are based on the b coefficient) for the pre- and post-usage data by going to the **Main Menu** and selecting **View Raw Data (Pre)** or **View Raw Data (Post)**.

Scaled preference ratings and data about the brand last purchased prior to advertising exposure and the simulated shopping experience

Resp. ID	Last Brand Bought	Agree	Wella B.	Flex	Sassoon	L'Oreal	Clairol	Enhance
1	5	1.835	1.416	0.709	1.056	1.916	2.538	0
2	6	0.769	0	0	0	0	1.354	0
3	6	1.236	0	1.825	0	0	3.338	0
4	1	4.67	0	1.774	0	0	0	0
5	2	1.94	4.158	1.152	1.955	4.12	4.961	0
6	1	4.432	3.568	2.757	3.134	0.458	2.314	0
7	4	2.258	3.017	3.509	4.705	0	1.232	0
8	5	1.868	1.636	0.974	0	2.231	0	0
9	4	0	4.472	3.339	1.863	4.605	1.432	0
10	1	3.724	0	0.704	0	0	0	0
11	5	0.99	4.646	0.355	0.166	4.826	3.16	0
12	6	1.355	0	0.65	0	0	3.171	0
13	1	3.784	0.87	2.475	1.445	1.866	2.507	0
14	4	2.347	0	0.252	4.804	0	0	0
15	1	3.411	0	1.316	0.487	3.008	2.074	0
16	2	4.768	4.784	4.71	1.389	1.109	0.418	0

References

Harvard Business School, "Johnson Wax: Enhance (A)," HBS Case #583046, © 1982, pp. 1-32.

Silk, Alvin J. and Urban, Glen L. 1978, "Pre-test Market Evaluation of New Packaged Goods: A Model and Measurement Methodology," *Journal of Marketing Research*, Vol. 15, No. 2 (May), pp. 171-191.

Urban, Glen L. and Katz, Gerald M. 1983, "Pre-test Market Models: Validation and Managerial Implications," *Journal of Marketing Research*, Vol. 20, No. 3 (August), pp. 221-234.

JOHNSON WAX: ENHANCE (A) CASE[*]

Instant hair conditioner

In April 1979, John Sherman, product development manager for S. C. Johnson & Company, was facing a decision on the future of Enhance, a new instant hair conditioner designed as a companion product to Agree, the company's first hair-care product. Development of Enhance had been under way for about a year and a half.

During the development process, Enhance had been tested against the leading existing products through blind comparisons and had undergone a pre-test-market testing procedure called ASSESSOR. The results of these tests would need to play a significant role in Sherman's recommendations, because previous experience had convinced top management that such research was valuable. In fact, the company had performed a number of ASSESSOR or similar analyses in the past, and top management had on occasion seemed anxious to skip the test market and push for introduction when the ASSESSOR results were favorable.

John Sherman's task was to recommend the next steps for Enhance. While his experience and intuitive judgment would be valued, he knew the managerial climate at S. C. Johnson would require marketing research substantiation for his recommendations.

S. C. Johnson & Company

S. C. Johnson & Company, headquartered in Racine, Wisconsin, was founded in 1886 as a manufacturer of parquet flooring. It was incorporated as S. C. Johnson & Son, Inc. and was familiarly known throughout the world as "Johnson Wax." A privately held corporation, Johnson Wax did not publicly report sales or earnings. Still, it was recognized as one of the world's leading manufacturers of products for home, auto and personal care, for commercial maintenance and industrial markets, and for outdoor recreation and leisure-time activities. Johnson Wax and its subsidiaries employed more than 13,000 people worldwide.

The buildings that served as international headquarters had been designed by Frank Lloyd Wright. They had won numerous architectural awards, and were listed in the National Register of Historic Places. U.S. manufacturing operations were conducted at the company's Waxdale, Wisconsin manufacturing plant, about eight miles west of Racine. This plant encompassed more than 1.9 million square feet of floor space and was one of the largest and most modern facilities of its kind in the world.

Johnson Wax maintained sales offices and sales and distribution centers in 20 major U.S. metropolitan areas.

Johnson Wax Associates, Inc. (JWA) was a group of nine associated companies that manufactured and marketed products for leisure-time activities and outdoor recreation. JWA products were distributed nationally and overseas to wholesalers and retailers through a system of manufacturers' representatives and factory salesmen.

The first Johnson Wax overseas subsidiary was established in England, in 1914. In 1979, Johnson Wax had subsidiaries in 45 countries.

The Johnson Wax consumer product line consisted of some of the best-known brands in household, automobile and personal-care products: Brite, Future, Glo-Coat, and Klear floor waxes; Jubilee and Pledge furniture polish, Rain Barrel Fabric Softener, Shout Stain Remover, Glory Carpet Cleaner, Glade Air Freshener, J-Wax auto care products, Raid insecticide, and Off insect repellent.

The Johnson Wax Innochem Division manufactured and distributed a complete line of heavy-duty polishes, cleaners, insecticides and disinfectants for use by commercial and institutional customers and a specialty line of chemicals.

The U.S. consumer products were distributed to supermarkets and drug, discount, and variety outlets through the company's own national sales force. Innochem commercial products distribution was handled through a separate sales force and through a network of more than 400 distributors nationally. Warehouse and distribution facilities were shared by the Innochem and Consumer Products Divisions.

New-product development at Johnson Wax

Development of these numerous product lines over the years had given Johnson Wax considerable experience in new-product evaluation and introduction. New product ideas came from laboratory research, marketing research, and customer contact. The product development process at Johnson Wax was fairly standard: ideas went through various commercial feasibility studies, performance tests against competitive products, and test markets before national introduction or rollout.

In recent years developing a new consumer product had become so expensive that Johnson Wax, like other manufacturers, had sought ways to reduce the cost. One solution was the pre-test-market test. One source[*] estimated the expected benefit from a $50,000 pretest to be in excess of $1 million. Before the Enhance pretest, Johnson Wax had performed many such pretests, most of them ASSESSORS.

The hair conditioning market

During the 1970s, both the variety and the number of hair-care products and brands had increased drastically. Shampoos to combat dandruff were introduced; others were custom-formulated for use on dry, normal, or oily hair. During the same period, new products were introduced that would "condition" hair as well as clean it. According to one manufacturer:

> A good creme rinse conditioner can help combat many hair problems. Hair can be easily damaged when it is combed following a shampoo, since hair is weakest when wet. Washing and towel-drying hair tend to tangle it, making it susceptible to breakage during combing. A creme rinse conditioner helps prevent this type of damage because it helps prevent tangles and makes for easy wet-combing. Creme rinse and conditioners also make hair feel softer; add to its bounce, shine, and body; and help prevent the buildup of static electricity that causes hair to be "flyaway."

There were two types of hair conditioners:

- ***Instant conditioners***, which were usually left on the hair for one to five minutes before being rinsed off.
- ***Therapeutic conditioners***, which generally remained on the hair from five to twenty minutes before rinsing.

The term "creme rinse" was still used occasionally for conditioners that stressed easier combing and manageability. Gradually, the term was being replaced by "instant conditioner." Hair conditioner sales had grown dramatically during the 1970s, spurred by new-product introductions and increased use, especially among young women.

The major instant hair conditioner brands and their market shares in 1978 were Johnson's Agree (15.2 percent), Wella Balsam (4.7 percent),

---

[*] Glen L. Urban and John R. Hauser, *Design and Marketing of New Products* (Englewood Cliffs, NJ: Prentice-Hall, Inc., 1980), pp. 52–59. The cost of a 9 month, two-market test market was estimated at about $1MM. The expected savings of ASSESSOR, although also $1MM, are computed from a Bayesian analysis involving: (1) costs of ASSESSOR, test markets, and national introduction; (2) probabilities of success at various stages of the new-product introduction process.

Clairol Condition (9.9 percent), Flex (13.4 percent), Tame (5.4 percent), and Sassoon.

Manufacturers' sales were as follows:

Manufacturers' Sales ($ millions)

Year	Total Conditioner	Instant Conditioner
1975	$132	$116
1976	160	141
1977	200	176
1978	230	202

Instant conditioners were sold in a variety of packages, but generally in either clear or opaque plastic bottles, often with nozzle tops. Popular sizes were 8-, 12-, and 16-ounce bottles. Retail margins generally ranged between 30 and 38 percent.

Agree

In June 1977, Johnson Wax entered the hair-care market with Agree Creme Rinse and Conditioner, soon followed by Agree Shampoo. At that time some creme rinses and conditioners included oil in their formulation. Agree's selling proposition was that the addition of this oil, especially for people with oily hair, caused the hair to look oily, greasy, and limp soon after shampooing. A technological breakthrough by Johnson Wax enabled it to produce a virtually oil-free product (Agree) which helped "stop the greasies." According to Johnson Wax promotional material:

> Agree has exceptional detangling properties making the hair easier to wet-comb. It is pleasantly scented and leaves the hair feeling clean, with healthy shine, bounce, and body. Agree contains no harsh or harmful ingredients and is pH balanced to be compatible with the natural pH of hair and scalp.

Agree had fared well in product comparison tests and an ASSESSOR pre-test-market test. By 1978, Agree had a 4.5 percent share of the shampoo market and 15.2 percent share of the conditioner market.

Enhance product development

Agree's early success created optimism and euphoria at Johnson Wax. Gaining a foothold in the attractive conditioner market offered an opportunity to expand the conditioner product line and subsequently make greater inroads on the even larger shampoo market.

Management felt Agree was successful largely because it solved a specific hair problem for a segment of the market. They also felt that it would be desirable to offer another personal-care product line. Enhance was conceived as an instant hair conditioner targeted toward women 25–45 years old with dry hair, and was formulated to appeal to that audience. Blind paired comparisons were run against Revlon's Flex.

The study, conceived by John Sherman and Neil Ford, of marketing research department, was summarized as follows:

> The purpose of the study was to determine the preference levels for Enhance, both overall and on specific performance attributes, versus those of Flex, the leading instant hair conditioner. A panel of 400 hair conditioner users was preselected by telephone. Each received both Enhance and Flex, blind-labeled and in identical nonidentifiable packages and, following proper rotations, used first one for three weeks, and the other for an identical period. At the end of the six-week usage period, respondents were interviewed regarding their preferences and behavior regarding the test products. A key part of the analysis was to determine preferences of women with specific hair care problems relevant to Enhance strategy and positioning.

A digest of the results appears in Exhibits 1 and 2. The conclusions drawn by Ford in an August 1978 report to Sherman were that:

> Differences between the two products are not great, but where they exist, they tend to be focused on the problems Enhance wishes to address and on the women to whom the brand will be targeted. While work should continue to improve the product, it is suitable for use in ASSESSOR in its current state and, if need be, for use in test-market introduction.

The ASSESSOR pre-test market

Following the blind comparison tests, further work on product formulation, product positioning, packaging, and advertising copy produced an introductory marketing plan. Advertising copy presented Enhance as a solution to the dry and damaged hair problem. Enhance samples were produced in "regular" and "extra conditioning" formulas.

When the marketing plan was agreed upon and samples were available, an ASSESSOR pre-test-market procedure was arranged. The primary objectives were to estimate the ongoing market share of Enhance and determine consumer reaction to the product. Two independent techniques were used to arrive at a market share prediction one year after introduction. The observed trial and repeat levels were used to make one share prediction. Another was made from estimates of brand preference calculated from the respondents' perception of, and preference for, the attributes of Enhance and the existing brands. Additional qualitative and quantitative information gathered during the laboratory phase, and again after use, added support for the primary conclusions of the ASSESSOR study.

ASSESSOR*, developed in 1973 by Management Decision Systems (MDS), of Waltham, Massachusetts, was one of a number of commercial simulated test-market procedures. The first was the Yankelovich Laboratory Test Market begun in 1968. Elrick and Lavidges' COMP, National Purchase Diary's ESP, and Burke Marketing Research's BASES followed, and by 1979, nearly 1400 applications of these models had been completed.

The Enhance ASSESSOR consisted of a laboratory and a callback phase. During the *laboratory phase*, women were intercepted in shopping malls and asked if they would participate in a test market. Those who were willing and were found to be in the target segment went through a five-step procedure, as follows:

1. *An initial questionnaire* was used to determine the brands about which the respondent could provide meaningful information. This list of brands, called the respondent's "evoked set," included brands used recently or ever, and brands that would, or would not, be considered on the next purchase occasion.

2. *The preference questionnaire* was customized for each respondent to include only those brands in her evoked set. The respondent was asked to allocate 11 imaginary chips between each pair of brands in her evoked set. These allocations were used to calculate the strength of preference for each brand in each respondent's evoked set. If there were N brands, the respondent was asked to give allocations for each of the $N(N-1)2$ pairs.

3. *Advertising recall* was measured after the respondent was shown commercials for six creme rinse/conditioning products: Tame, Agree, Flex, Condition, Wella Balsam, and Enhance.

4. *Laboratory purchasing* took place in a simulated store where the respondent was given a $2.25 certificate. If she wanted to buy more than $2.25 in merchandise, she was asked to pay the difference. Respondents who did not purchase Enhance were given a package of Enhance as a gift. Half the nonpurchasers received a 2 oz. container, the other half received an 8 oz. container. A limited number of those who did not purchase the test product were asked a few additional questions probing their impressions of Enhance and reasons for not purchasing it.

---

* More detailed descriptions of ASSESSOR may be found in the appendix to this case and in Alvin J. Silk and Glen L. Urban, "Pre-Test-Market Evaluation of New Packaged Goods: A Model and Measurement Methodology," *Journal of Marketing Research*, Vol. XV (May 1978), pp. 171-191.

5. *Brand ratings.* Respondents were then asked to rate several of their evoked brands on how well they performed on 22 product attributes. Enhance was also rated on these attributes. These ratings, since the respondent had not used Enhance, were based on perceptions created through advertising, price, and packaging. A 7-point rating scale was used.

The *callback phase* was designed to collect information about after-use preferences, repeat purchase rate, and diagnostics concerning product performance. Only those respondents who indicated they had used Enhance were asked to complete the interview. Callback interviews were conducted four weeks after the laboratory interview.

The field research was conducted in three markets—Atlanta, Chicago, and Denver—beginning September 25, 1978, with callback interviews approximately four weeks later. A total of 387 interviews was conducted with users of creme rinse/conditioning products. Respondents included 120 users of Agree creme rinse, a disproportionate number, in order to better determine Enhance's effect on Agree.

ASSESSOR results

ASSESSOR provided results in eight major areas of interest: (1) market structure, (2) advertising recall, (3) trial, (4) repeat purchase, (5) product acceptance, (6) market share prediction, (7) cannibalization, and (8) sampling response.

1. **Market Structure**: During the laboratory phase of the field-work, respondents were asked to rate several of their evoked brands as well as their "ideal" brand on 22 attributes. These brand ratings were used as inputs to factor analysis[*], a data-reduction technique used for grouping similar attributes into underlying factors or dimensions. From this analysis, four basic perceptual dimensions, or factors, emerged:

---

[*] See Appendix A for description of factor analysis procedure.

Factor	Relative Importance	Attributes Combined to Form the Factor
Conditioning	33%	Nourishes dry hair
		Restores moisture
		Keeps control of split ends
		Makes dry hair healthy looking
		Conditions hair
		Helps keep hair from breaking
		Penetrates hair
Clean	27%	Leaves hair free of residue/flakes
		Leaves hair grease- and oil-free
		Leaves hair clean looking
		Rinses out easily/completely
Manageability/effects	23%	Makes hair more manageable
		Leaves hair shiny/lustrous
		Leaves hair soft and silky
		Gives hair body and fullness
Fragrance	17%	Has pleasant fragrance while using
		Leaves hair with nice fragrance

Besides identifying the possible factors underlying the instant conditioner market, factor analysis provided a graphic representation of the consumer's positioning of the brands in a "perceptual map." This was done by using pairs of factors as axes and assigning each brand a "factor score" that served as a coordinate on each axis. Using these coordinates, a brand was assigned a position on the perceptual map. MDS produced perceptual maps for a number of market segments. The maps for the total market are shown in Exhibit 3. (Maps including the fragrance factor are not presented.)

MDS's report concluded that, in terms of market structure,

> The fact that all four dimensions are important to all consumers' segments considered in the study suggests that being strongly positioned on only one dimension may not be sufficient to capture a significant portion of the market.

> Agree and Breck Creme Rinse have achieved the "clean" position, while Clairol Condition has succeeded in differentiating itself as the "conditioning" brand. Wella Balsam, based on these maps, appears to have virtually no image, and thus might be vulnerable to a new entry. Sassoon, a relatively new brand, appears to be enjoying a very strong positive image.

2. **Advertising Recall**: Unaided advertising recall provided a measure of how well an ad broke through the clutter of competitive advertising. Total unaided recall for Enhance was 76 percent, about aver-

age for ASSESSOR-tested products, but somewhat lower than for other Johnson Wax products subjected to ASSESSOR tests. Unaided recall did not differ across hair type segments.

Among those who recalled the Enhance ad, almost 50 percent recalled that Enhance was "for dry hair." "Conditions" and "penetrates" received somewhat lower playback. Exhibit 4 summarizes the copypoint recall results.

3. **Trial Estimation**: Store setups had been designed to reflect local conditions and simulate the anticipated competitive environment. Enhance was available in two sizes for both regular and extra conditioning formulations. Enhance had one facing for each size and formulation, and was featured in the middle of the middle shelf. In all, 24 shampoos and conditioners were represented in 60 facings. Enhance was offered in 8 and 16 ounce sizes at $1.31 and $1.94, respectively. Agree was offered in 8 and 12 ounce sizes at $1.31 and $1.67. Flex was offered only in the 16 ounce size at the same price as Agree. Enhance prices were very similar to those of Breck, Wella Balsam, and Tame.

Trial was measured as a percentage of total laboratory purchasing. Of the 387 respondents, 307 (79 percent) made a purchase in the store. Enhances trial rate was 23 percent. Agree had achieved an overall trial rate of 33 percent in its ASSESSOR test. For purposes of comparison, Exhibit 5 shows trial rates for other ASSESSOR-tested products, both within and outside the health and beauty aids category.

4. **Repeat Purchase Estimation**: Repeat purchase and product acceptance were determined through telephone callback interviews four weeks after the laboratory interviews. Since all respondents who had not purchased Enhance were given samples, after-use data were potentially available for all respondents. Those who had not used Enhance were not asked to complete the phone interview. Telephone callbacks were completed with 215 respondents (55 percent of all laboratory respondents). This was lower than most ASSESSOR callback completion rates. Of those people with whom callback interviews were *not* completed, 23 percent (42 people) indicated they had not used Enhance because it was specifically formulated for dry hair.

During the callback interviews, respondents were again asked to compare Enhance with other brands in their evoked sets. This information was used to see whether use altered Enhance's position in the market structure (Enh. Post in Exhibit 3).

Respondents were also given the opportunity to purchase another bottle of Enhance at the prices found in the laboratory store. Those who decided to repurchase, plus those who said without prompting that their next conditioner purchase would be Enhance, were classified as repeaters. Repeat rates were as follows:

	Enhance	**Agree**
Repeat among buyers in laboratory	60%	78%
Repeat among nonbuyers (who received sample)	43	63

72 percent of those repeating purchased Enhance's "Extra Conditioning Formula" and 64 percent purchased the 16 ounce size.

The repeat purchase rates of other ASSESSOR-tested products are found in Exhibit 6.

5. ***Product Acceptance***: During the callback interview the respondent was asked what she liked best about Enhance. Surprisingly, manageability, not conditioning, was mentioned most frequently, even though it was not considered a main copy point. Those who made a repeat purchase were even more likely than nonrepeaters to mention manageability. Open ended likes and dislikes for Enhance are found in Exhibit 7. Exhibit 8 presents after-use preferences and comparisons with users' favorite brands.

6. ***Market Share Prediction***: A major feature that differentiated ASSESSOR from other pretest market procedures was the use of two convergent methods to predict market share. Market share was estimated separately with a "trial and repeat" model and a "preference" model.

Trial and repeat model

The trial and repeat model used the purchase information gathered during laboratory shopping and follow-up interview repeat measurements. The formula used was

$$M = TS$$

where

$M =$ market share,

$T =$ the ultimate cumulative trial rate (penetration or trial),

$S =$ the ultimate repeat purchase rate among those buyers who have ever made a trial purchase of the brand (retention).

Retention (S) was a function of the initial repeat purchase rate and the rate at which previous triers returned to Enhance after buying another product (called switchback). The relationship is explained in Appendix A.

As mentioned above, Enhance obtained a laboratory trial of 23 percent, and a repeat rate of 60 percent. Measured through a series of callback interviews, the switchback rate was 16 percent. Retention was calculated to be 28.6 percent. Since these estimates were achieved in an environment in which every respondent was aware of Enhance advertising, and Enhance was always available, corrections had to be made to adjust these laboratory measurements to actual market conditions. Market trial was estimated by

$$T \ = \ FKD + CU - \{(FKD) \times (CU)\}$$

where

F = the trial rate in the ASSESSOR test—the trial rate that would ultimately occur if all consumers were aware of the advertising.

K = the long-run probability that a consumer will become aware of Enhance.

D = the proportion of retail outlets that will ultimately carry Enhance.

C = the proportion of the target market that receives samples.

U = the proportion of those receiving samples that will use them.

Using CU to estimate the trial resulting from sampling, would overstate the extent of sampling trial, since some trial would have resulted from advertising even without sampling. This "overlap" trial $((FKD) \times (CU))$ would be double-counted, and must therefore be subtracted from the sample-induced trial rate.

The market share estimates for Enhance depended not only on data obtained from the ASSESSOR test, but also on John Sherman's estimates of what advertising awareness and distribution levels would be realized for Enhance. Sherman had decided to initially use the advertising awareness and distribution levels realized for Agree:

awareness	70%
distribution	85%

Using these values, and ignoring sampling for the moment, market share was predicted by the trial/repeat model at 3.9 percent. Sherman's computations of Enhance market share, together with those for Agree, are found in Exhibit 9.

Preference model estimates of share

The preference model market share prediction was based on the respondents' answers to the questions about product attributes and the degree to which they perceived these attributes to be present in competing brands. The preference model predicted that Enhance would attain a 27.5 percent share of those consumers in whose evoked sets it appeared. Using the penetration rate found in the laboratory phase of the ASSESSOR study (14 percent), MDS obtained a base market share estimate of 3.8 percent (see Exhibit 9).

7. **Cannibalization**: An estimate of the cannibalization of Agree's share was also computed from the ASSESSOR results by computing Enhance's share separately for Agree users. This analysis demonstrated that Enhance would draw less than proportionately from Agree, with only a share of 2.4 percent among Agree users. This indicated that Agree would lose less than half a share point to Enhance.

More detailed analysis indicated that Enhance would draw more than proportionately to share from Wella Balsam, proportionately to share from Flex and Sassoon, and less than proportionately from Agree, L'Oreal, and Clairol Condition.

8. **Incremental Share from Sampling**: The incremental share that might be expected from sampling could be estimated, since those respondents who had not chosen Enhance had been given a sample of the product at the end of the initial ASSESSOR interview. Their use and acceptance levels were determined during the callback interview.

The effects of sampling were evaluated by first determining the incremental trial rate that would result from sampling. Of those using samples, a certain percentage (equal to net cumulative trial) would have tried the product anyway; the remainder were new triers due to sampling. (See formula above.) These incremental triers would now follow the normal switching process, and their long-run share potential could be estimated like that for the advertising induced triers. These calculations, found in Exhibit 10, estimated or incremental 2 percent share from a 35 million sample drop. Considering the effect of sampling, market share was estimated at 5.8 percent by the preference model and 5.9 percent by the trial/repeat model.

9. **Volume Predictions**: As a final step in the evaluation of Enhance's success potential, it was necessary to convert the share estimates into dollar sales projections. Doing this required a number of additional

facts and adjustments. The 1979 volume of instant hair conditioner sales was projected to be $250 million. To find the volume that would result from a given Enhance share, it would be necessary to adjust the share for price and frequency-of-use differences between Enhance and the average for the category.

A use adjustment based on expected source of volume and frequency of use, indicated that Enhance's frequency of use would be about 0.9 times the category average. The tested Enhance prices and share of sales accounted for by the two sizes resulted in a price adjustment of 1.04. Multiplying these two adjustment factors resulted in a factor of 0.94 to be used to convert unit market share to dollar share.

Volume was then predicted, according to the two models, as follows:

	Trial/Repeat Model	**Preference Model**
Manufacturer's Category Volume	$250MM	$250MM
Enhance Unit Share	3.90%	3.80%
Enhance Dollar Share (Unit Share * .94)	3.66%	3.57%
Enhance Sales	$9.15MM	$8.93MM
Additional Sales From Promotion		
Promotion Unit Share	2.0	
Promotion Dollar Share	1.88	
Enhance Sales	4.7MM	4.7MM
Total Sales	$13.85MM	$13.63MM

Recommendations

MDS, as a result of the ASSESSOR study, was not encouraging about Enhance's prospects. It also thought sampling would not be successful for Enhance. Johnson Wax management had set a market share of 10 percent.[*]

John Sherman knew, however, that the final recommendations were his to make. He could recommend that Enhance be abandoned; reformulated; and/or retested; or that a national rollout begin. The final decision lay somewhere higher up in the organization, but his recommendations would be considered carefully.

---

[*] As a privately held corporation, Johnson Wax did not report financial data publicly. Manufacturers of health and beauty aids in general held cost data close to their chests. Exhibit 11 displays some approximate information on industry cost structure. The data are included for discussion purposes only and should not be considered indicative of Enhance's actual cost structure.

Blind Use Test Results

Incidence of Problems

	All Women	25-29	30-34	35 or Older
Dry/Damage Problems	53%	55%	53%	46%
Split ends	34	42	35	29
Dryness	32	29	35	31
Brittle/breaking	12	13	17	9
Damaged hair	13	10	18	11
Dull/Limp Problems	65%	64%	68%	58%
Hard to manage	38	32	42	39
Dull/no shine	24	16	21	30
Fine/limp hair	44	45	39	46

Each respondent was screened for the presence of any of these seven hair problems. The seven problems, in turn, were subjectively grouped into those to do with "Dry/Damage" and those to do with "Dull/Limp."

Overall Preference

	(BASE)	Prefer Enhance	Prefer Flex	No Difference
ALL USERS	(320)	48%	44%	8%
By Age				
Under 35	(166)	46	47	7
35 or over	(154)	50	40	10
By Hair Type				
Oily	(94)	51	45	4
Normal	(154)	44	47	9
Dry	(72)	53*	35	12
By Hair Quality				
Dry/damaged–net	(168)	50*	40	10
Fine/limp–net	(208)	49*	43	8

*Significant at 90 percent confidence level.

EXHIBIT 1

Johnson Wax: ENHANCE (A)

Blind Use Test Results (continued)

Preference on Specific Attributes

	Prefer Enhance	Prefer Flex	No Difference
Fragrance			
In bottle	27%	32%	41%
While using	34	37	29
After dry	28	28	44
Feels Cleaner			
While using	18	17	65
When dry	26*	19	55
Next day	26	22	52
Conditioning			
Conditioning	28	24	48
Softer	31	26	43
Body	31	32	37
More manageable	32	30	38
Better shine	14	16	70
Relieves dryness	(22)	15	63
Combing			
Easy to comb	22	20	58
Tangle free	16	16	68
Use/Application			
Applies evenly	(30)	14	56
Penetrates better	(28)	18	54
Rinses out easier	22	21	57
Product			
Better color	4	6	90
Better consistency	27	29	44

BASE: 320 Users

( )   Significant at 95 percent C.L
*   Significant at 90 percent C.L.

EXHIBIT 2

Johnson Wax: ENHANCE (A)

ASSESSOR results
Product map

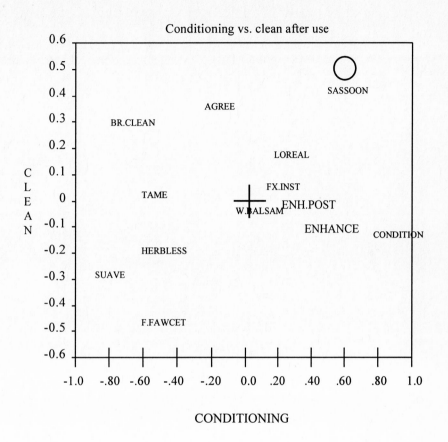

ENHANCE = Before positioning.
ENH.POST = After-use positioning.
I = Ideal brand positioning.

EXHIBIT 3
Johnson Wax: Enhance (A)

ASSESSOR results
Product map

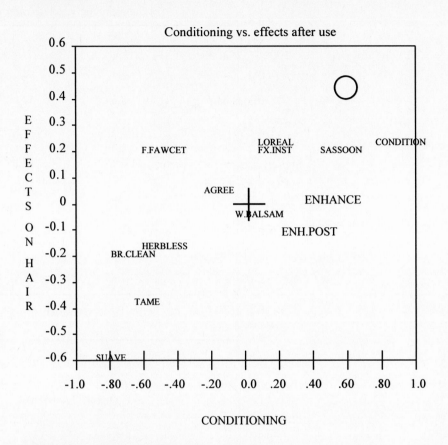

ENHANCE = Before positioning.
ENH.POST = After-use positioning.
I = Ideal brand positioning.

EXHIBIT 3 cont'd.
Johnson Wax: Enhance (A)

ASSESSOR Results

Copy Point Recall

	Overall	Buyer	Nonbuyer
For Dry Hair			
Good for dry hair	46.8%	50.0%	46.1%
Nourishes hair	33.1	37.9	32.0
Prevents dry hair	5.4	1.7	6.2
Doesn't leave hair dry	0.7	0.0	0.8
Conditions	20.4%	27.6%	18.7%
Conditions hair	8.0	17.2	5.8
Good for damaged hair	5.4	5.2	5.4
Repairs hair	4.0	6.9	3.3
For brittle hair	3.3	1.7	3.7
Protects from heat damage	0.7	0.0	0.8
Mends split ends	0.7	0.0	0.8
Penetrates	19.7%	31.0%	17.0%
Penetrates hair	19.7	31.0	17.0
Doesn't just coat hair	3.3	8.6	2.1
Manageability	11.4%	17.2%	10.0%
Makes hair more manageable	7.7	12.1	6.6
Good for limp hair	3.3	3.4	3.3
Eliminates tangles	0.7	1.7	0.4
Texture of Hair	6.4%	5.2%	6.6%
Gives hair more body/bounce	4.3	1.7	5.0
Leaves hair soft	2.0	3.4	1.7
BASE:	(299)	(58)	(241)

EXHIBIT 4

Johnson Wax: ENHANCE (A)

Trial Comparison to all ASSESSOR-tested health and beauty aids products

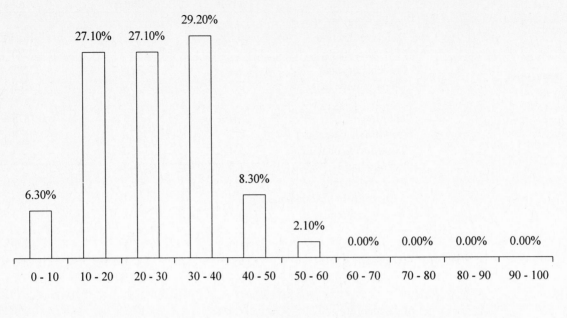

% TRIAL

Trial comparison to all ASSESSOR-tested products

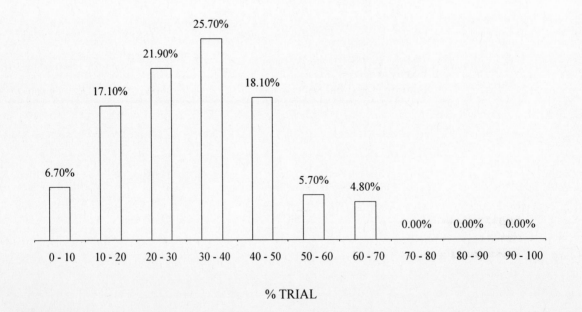

% TRIAL

EXHIBIT 5
Johnson Wax: ENHANCE (A)

Repeat comparison to all ASSESSOR-tested health and beauty aids products

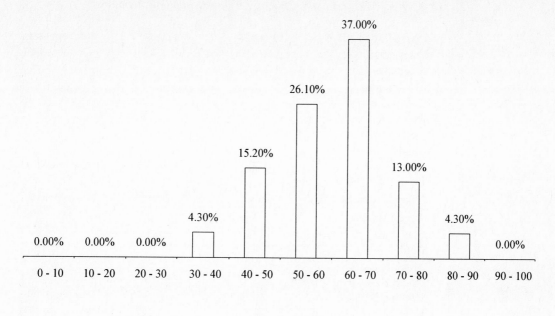

% REPEAT

Repeat comparison to all ASSESSOR-tested products

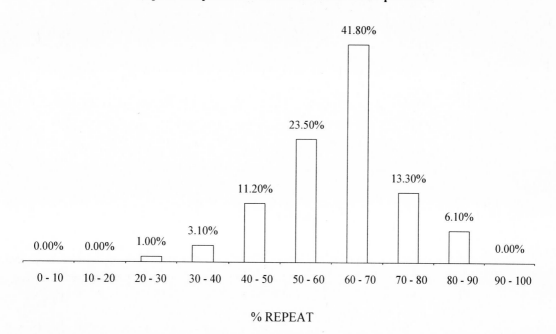

% REPEAT

EXHIBIT 6
Johnson Wax: ENHANCE (A)

ASSESSOR Results

Open-Ended Likes and Dislikes for Enhance (multiple mentions)

Open-Ended Likes	Overall	Repeaters	Nonrepeaters
Manageability	42%	48%	37%
Fragrance	21	14	27
Conditioning	11	12	10
Consistency	7	7	6
Application/ease of use	7	6	7
Penetrates	6	5	7
Clean	5	7	4
Base	(215)	(102)	(113)

Open-Ended Dislikes	Overall	Repeaters	Nonrepeaters
Manageability	24%	9%	38%
Fragrance	16	7	25
Conditioning	11	8	13
Consistency	1	3	0
Application/ease of use	1	1	1
Nothing Disliked	59	74	46
Base	(215)	(102)	(113)

EXHIBIT 7
Johnson Wax: ENHANCE (A)

ASSESSOR Results

After-Use Preferences

	Percent Prefer Enhance*				
	1st	2nd	3rd	4th	(Base)
Dry Hair	38	32	17	7	(93)
Oily Hair	22	34	20	15	(41)
Normal	23	34	19	12	(69)
Total Sample	28	33	19	11	(215)
Total Sample (Agree)	54	26	12	2	(279)

Comparison to Regular Brand

		Among Triers	*Among Nontriers*	
	Enhance (%)	Agree (%)	Enhance (%)	Agree (%)
Much better	30	44	14	35
A little better	24	25	21	22
About the same	26	13	37	21
A little poorer	14	12	16	13
Much poorer	6	5	12	8
(Base)	(50)	(76)	(165)	(203)

*To be read, of the 93 respondents with dry hair, 38 percent rated Enhance as their favorite brand, for 32 percent it was their second choice, etc.

EXHIBIT 8
Johnson Wax: ENHANCE (A)

ASSESSOR Results
Market Share Prediction Trial Repeat Model

		Enhance	**Agree**
1.	Trial	23%	33%
2.	Awareness from advertising and sampling	.70	.70
3.	Distribution	.85	.85
4.	Net cumulative trial $[(1) \times (2) \times (3)]$	13.7%	19.6%
5.	Repeat	.60	.78
6.	Switchback	.16	.15
7.	Share of triers' choices $\left[\frac{6}{1+(6)-5}\right]$ (retention)	28.6%	41%
8.	Base share $[(4) \times (7)]$	3.9%	8.1

Preference Model

		Enhance	**Agree**
9.	Share for Enhance if everyone evokes it	27.5%	42.0%
10.	Estimated penetration [equal to (4)]	.14	.20
11.	Base share	3.8%	8.4%

EXHIBIT 9
Johnson Wax. ENHANCE (A)

ASSESSOR Results
Estimated Incremental Share from Sampling
for 35 Million Sample Drop with 90 Percent Delivery

Enhance vs. Agree
1. Number of samples delivered $[35M \times .9]$	31.5MM
2. Percent hitting target group	80%
3. Percent used*	60%
4. Number of samples used $[(1) \times (2) \times (3)]$	15.12MM
5. Percent using samples* $[(4) \div 6OMM \text{ households}]$	25%
6. Overlap $[(5) \times \text{Trial Rate Advertising (line 4, Ex. 9)}]$	3%
7. Net incremental trial $[(5)—(6)]$	22%
8. First repeat* (repeat among nonbuyers)	43%
9. Share of triers' choices (retention)	22%
10. Incremental share from sampling $[(7) \times (8) \times (9)]$	2.0%

*Measured through ASSESSOR callbacks.

**Calculated from formula $\dfrac{SB}{1 + SB - R}$ where SB is given in line 6 of Exhibit 9
and R is line 8 of this exhibit.

EXHIBIT 10
Johnson Wax: ENHANCE (A)

Approximate Health and Beauty Aid Industry Cost Structures*
(Indexed to Suggested Retail Price)

Suggested retail price	100
Expected shelf price (large 16 oz.)	83
(small 8 oz.)	73
Manufacturer's selling price	56
Cost of goods sold	21%

*These data are not supplied by the Johnson Wax Company, and are not known to be indicative of its actual costs. They are thought to reflect the average market cost structure closely enough to be helpful in the case discussion

EXHIBIT 11
Johnson Wax: ENHANCE (A)

APPENDIX A
Johnson Wax: Enhance (A)

Market share prediction models

The market share prediction in ASSESSOR was calculated from two independent models.

1. The trial and repeat model was based on:
   trial (measured in the laboratory store), repeat (measured in the callback interview), switchback (measured in multiple call backs).

2. The preference model was based on:
   after-use preferences for the test product (callback), the relationship between preferences and purchasing behavior in the specific market (laboratory).

A convergence between the predictions of these two models serves to increase confidence in the final market share prediction.

Trial and repeat model

The target market for the product is represented by the respondents chosen in the ASSESSOR test. In the test procedure, some respondents buy Enhance in the laboratory store. The proportion of buyers provides an estimate of trial, which must be corrected for probable awareness and availability in the actual marketplace. This corrected trial level is used to estimate the *cumulative* penetration the test product will achieve in the real market. Once cumulative penetration has been estimated, it is necessary to estimate the number of purchases that will be generated on an ongoing basis. This is called "retention," and is a function of the amount of brand switching that will occur.

At any given time, t, the purchasers of instant hair conditioners could be segmented into two groups—those who bought Enhance last time and those who didn't. What could happen at time $t+1$ is illustrated below. Of those who bought Enhance at time $t(X)$, some will also buy it at $t+1$, their next purchase occasion (R), whereas others will buy a competitive brand (X-R). At $t+1$ some of those who had bought Enhance before t, but didn't buy it at t, will switch back (SB). Others will continue to purchase a competing brand.

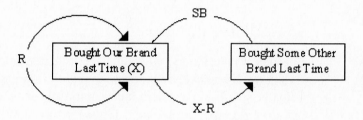

The customers who repeat plus those who don't repeat must equal 100 percent of those who bought the Enhance at their last purchase occasion. Similarly, switchback plus nonswitchback must equal 100 percent of those who bought Enhance at some time in the past, but not on the last purchase occasion. This is illustrated below.

Assume 100 consumers have tried Enhance. If the repeat rate is 81 percent[*] and the switchback rate 20 percent,[*] then on successive purchase occasions we would expect to observe the following:

Purchase Cycle	Eligible to Repeat	=	Repeat (R)	+	Do Not Repeat	Eligible to Switchback	=	Switchback (SB)	+	Do Not Switchback
1st	100.0		81.0		19.0	-		-		-
2nd	81.0		65.6		15.4	19.0		3.8		15.2
3rd	69.4		56.2		13.2	30.6		6.1		24.5
4th	62.3		50.5		11.8	37.7		7.5		30.2
5th	58.0		47.0		11.0	42.0		8.4		33.6
6th	55.4		44.9		10.5	44.6		8.9		35.7
7th	53.8		etc.		etc.	46.2		etc.		etc.

Now compute the percentage of triers who have purchased Enhance in any past period that will purchase it in the present period:

Purchase Cycle	Buy Enhance (R + SB)	Buy Other Brands
1st	81.0%	19.0%
2nd	69.4	30.6
3rd	62.3	37.7
4th	58.0	42.0
5th	55.4	44.6
6th	53.8	46.2
7th	52.8	47.2

*These values are used for illustration only.

Notice how the percentage of triers who will repurchase Enhance on a given occasion varies from the previous period value less and less as the number of purchase occasions increases. In fact, if we continued this sequence indefinitely, we would finally arrive at 51.3 percent, and this value would be called the retention rate. The value at which this process finally stabilizes is determined completely by the repeat rate and the switchback rate, so it is not necessary to calculate retention this way. This illustration is an example of what is called a two-stage Markov process. It is not critical to know any more about a two-stage Markov process to understand ASSESSOR than the formula for the final retention rate, or

$$S = \frac{SB}{1 + SB - R} \cdot *$$

*SB and R are expected to be decimal fractions, i.e., .3 instead of 30 percent.

We can compute retention quite simply by using this equation. If, for example, R = .50 and SB = .20, what would the retention rate be? We might also note that in our example, after only seven purchase occasions, we were getting quite close to .513.

The last step in the calculation is to compute market share as the product of penetration (the percentage who will try the product) and retention (the share of ongoing purchases by those who have tried the product).

Market share = penetration × retention.

To summarize, the procedure used to predict market share with the trial and repeat model is:

1. Measure trial in the laboratory.

2. Multiply this trial rate by expected awareness and availability to compute penetration in a nonlaboratory situation.
3. Measure repeat and switchback in the callback phase.
4. Use Markov formula to compute retention.
5. Multiply penetration by retention to get market share.

Preference model

The preference model for predicting market share is considerably more sophisticated in its derivation than is the trial and repeat model, and much of the detail is beyond the scope of this case. Those interested are directed to the Silk and Urban article referenced earlier.

An overview of the process is as follows:

Analysis of existing brands

1. From a respondent's chip allocations, described in the case, a preference score $V(j)$ is computed for each brand j. These preference scores are computed using a technique borrowed from mathematical psychology.

2. The next step is to use these estimated brand-preference scores to compute the probability of a brand j being purchased by a respondent, $P(j)$. The conversion formula is

$$P(j) = \frac{\hat{V}(j)^{\beta}}{\sum_{k}\left[\hat{V}(k)\right]^{\beta}}$$

where the summation is over the j brands in the respondent's evoked set.

These steps are taken to estimate the probability of purchase for the brands that existed in the market before Enhance was introduced. In this formulation, β is an estimate of the degree of brand loyalty in the market.

3. The chip allocation procedure is repeated during the callback phase of the ASSESSOR process. β is assumed to remain unchanged with the introduction and trial of Enhance, so the following equation estimates the probability that a consumer would choose Enhance after having tried it.

$$L(i) = \frac{A(i)^{\beta}}{A(i)^{\beta} + \sum_k (A(k))^{\beta}}$$

where

$A(i)$ = estimated preference of the consumer for Enhance after having tried it.

$A(k)$ = estimated preference of the consumer for brand k after having tried Enhance.

$\hat{\beta}$ = a parameter to be estimated.

Summation is over the brands in the consumer's evoked set.

These predicted brand preferences are computed for each consumer separately and are conditional on the evoked set of the consumer. Expected market shares could be computed for the brands by aggregating the individual brand preferences and multiplying by the proportion of consumers who would include Enhance in their evoked sets.

$$M(j) = E(j)\frac{\sum_{k=1}^{N} L_k(j)}{N}$$

where

$M(j)$ = expected market share for brand j.

$E(j)$ = proportion of consumers for whom brand j will be in their evoked set.

$L_k(j)$ = predicted probability of purchase of brand j by consumer k.

N = Number of consumers.

Factor analysis and market maps

Exhibit 3 displayed graphic representations of the relative location of existing and "ideal" brands. They were drawn using a technique called factor analysis. What follows is an intuitive idea of what factor analysis seeks to do and how these "maps" are drawn.

Suppose we had a set of six questions about the attributes of instant hair conditioners like these:

BRAND: _____

Please rate the above brand of creme rinse, hair conditioner, or balsam conditioning product on each of the items below. The *best possible* rating you can give is a 7, the *poorest possible rating* is a 1. Circle *one* number for each item listed. Even if you have never used the product yourself, we would like your impression of what it is like based on what you have seen or heard.

		Best Possible Rating						Poorest Possible Rating
1.	Nourishes dry hair	7	6	5	4	3	2	1
2.	Leaves hair free of residue, film, and flakes	7	6	5	4	3	2	1
3.	Gives hair body and fullness	7	6	5	4	3	2	1
4.	Rinses out easily/completely	7	6	5	4	3	2	1
5.	Restores moisture	7	6	5	4	3	2	1
6.	Keeps control of split ends	7	6	5	4	3	2	1
7.	Leaves hair feeling soft and silky	7	6	5	4	3	2	1

Each respondent would answer these questions about Enhance and the other brands in her evoked set. We would like to see whether there are consistent patterns of response to these questions, e.g., questions 1 and 5 both seem to have something to do with moisture, so we might expect a respondent to give a brand either high or low ratings on both questions. The degree to which questions are answered in similar ways is measured by a number called the "correlation coefficient."

The correlation coefficient simply measures the extent to which two questions are answered above or below their respective averages. If every respondent in this test gave higher than average responses to two questions, the correlation coefficient for those two questions would be 1. If every respondent's answer to one question was higher than the average response while the answer to the other question was always lower than the average, the correlation coefficient for the two questions would be −1. Correlation coefficients are always between these two extreme values. A correlation coefficient of 0 would mean there was no consistent pattern of response for the two questions.

Exhibit A1 is a display of correlation coefficients for the responses to the seven questions presented above.

Hypothetical correlation between responses to selected questions*

Question	1	2	3	4	5	6	7
1	1.						
2	.2	1.					
3	.1	-.1	1.				
4	-.3	.9	-.1	1.			
5	.8	-.2	.2	-.2	1.		
6	.7	-.1	.1	-.1	.9	1.	
7	.2	-.1	.8	.2	.1	.3	1.

EXHIBIT Al
Johnson Wax: ENHANCE (A)

*These are not the real correlations, but have been redesigned to illustrate a point.

If we look at the correlations between the responses to the seven questions, we can see that some of them seem to be related, e.g., responses to questions 1, 5 and 6 seem to go together; 2 and 4; and 3 and 7 go together. Let's rewrite Exhibit Al grouping these questions together.

Rearranged correlations between selected questions

Question	f_1 1	5	6	f_2 2	4	f_3 3	7
f_1 1	1.						
5	.8	1.					
6	.7	.9	1.				
f_2 2	.2	-.2	-.1	1.			
4	-.3	-.2	-.1	.9	1.		
3	.1	.2	.1	-.1	-.1	1	
f_3 7	.2	.1	.3	-.1	.2	.8	1

EXHIBIT A2
Johnson Wax: ENHANCE (A)

As you examine Exhibit A2, notice how we have three blocks of questions and in each block the correlations between responses to the questions are high, while the correlations between responses to questions in different blocks are low. Suppose we had a set of three uncorrelated variables. Their correlation array would look like this:

$$
\begin{array}{ccc}
1. & & \\
0 & 1. & \\
0 & 0 & 1.
\end{array}
$$

That is what Exhibit A2 looks like if you look just at the blocks and not the individual questions. If we considered each block to represent a variable, we would have a new set of variables called factors: factor 1 would consist of questions 1, 5 and 6; factor 2 would consist of questions 2 and 4; and factor 3 would consist of questions 3 and 7.

What are these new variables? We have to name them ourselves, but their properties are given by the questions that define them. In the case, factor 1 was called "conditioning"; factor 2 "cleaning"; and factor 3 "manageability/effects."

This exercise has been quite simplistic; the groupings were clear from the start. This isn't always the case. Frequently many questions are asked to explore consumers' perceptions of products and the underlying dimensions of the market are by no means obvious. Or perhaps a manager would just like to see whether her perception of the market is backed up by objective measurement. In either of these situations factor analysis is very helpful.

What does factor analysis do? It finds the subgrouping of a large set of variables in which the original variables are highly correlated within the subgroup, or factor, and least correlated between factors.

How are graphs like those in Exhibit 3 drawn? That's fairly easy. Each of the original questions (variables) has a coefficient, a_i, that relates it to the factor to which it belongs, much like a regression coefficient. So we can write:

$$ f_1 = a_0 + a_1 v_1 + a_2 v_2 + - - + a_k v_k $$

If we take the mean score attributed to each question for a given brand, we can use this equation to compute what is called the factor score f_1 for that brand. If we have three factors, we can compute three factor scores for each brand. Using these three factor scores, we can locate the brand in a three-dimensional space where each dimension represents a factor.

Chapter 6

TUTORIAL FOR THE GENERALIZED BASS MODEL (GBASS)

Concept

The Bass model for forecasting first purchase has had a long history in marketing. It is most appropriate for forecasting sales of an innovation (more generally, a new product) for which no closely competing alternatives exist in the marketplace.

The Bass model offers a good starting point for forecasting the long-term sales pattern of new technologies and new durable products under two types of conditions: (1) the firm has recently introduced the product or technology and has observed its sales for a few time periods; or (2) the firm has not yet introduced the product or technology, but it is similar in some way to existing products or technologies whose sales history is known. The model attempts to predict how many customers will eventually adopt the new product and when they will adopt.

Bass suggested that the likelihood ($L(t)$) that a customer will adopt an innovation at time t (given that the customer had not adopted before) could be characterized as:

$$L(t) = p + \frac{q}{\overline{N}} N(t),$$

where

$N(t)$ = the number of customers who have already adopted the innovation by time t;

$\overline{N}$ = a parameter representing the total number of customers in the adopting target segment, all of whom will eventually adopt the product;

p = coefficient of innovation (or coefficient of external influence); and

q = coefficient of imitation (or coefficient of internal influence).

The equation above suggests that the *likelihood* that a customer will adopt at time t is the sum of two components. The first component (p) refers to a constant propensity to adopt that is independent of how many other customers have adopted the innovation before time t. The second component [$(q/\overline{N})N(t)$] is proportional to the number of customers who have already adopted the innovation by time t and represents the extent of favorable interactions between the innovators and the other adopters of the product (imitators).

After transforming the above equation into one that looks at the number of adopters at t ($n(t)$) we get

$$n(t) = p\overline{N} + (q - p)N(t) - \frac{q}{N}[N(t)]^2 .$$

If $q > p$, then imitation effects dominate the innovation effects and the plot of $n(t)$ against time (t) will have an inverted U shape. This is likely to be the case for new movies, new records, or such new technologies as cellular radios. On the other hand, if $q > p$, then innovation effects will dominate and the highest sales will occur at introduction and sales will decline in every period after that (e.g., blockbuster movies). Furthermore, the lower the value of p, the longer it takes to realize sales growth for the innovation. When both p and q are large, product sales take off rapidly and fall off quickly after reaching a maximum.

Bass, Krishnan, and Jain (1994) proposed a general form of the equation that incorporates the effects of marketing-mix variables on the likelihood of adoption, so that by increasing marketing effort, a firm can increase the likelihood of adoption of the innovation—that is, marketing effort (increasing advertising or decreasing price) speeds up the rate of diffusion in the population.

Software

The Excel spreadsheet GBass implements the original Bass model (Bass 1969) as well as an extended version of it, the generalized Bass model (Bass, Krishnan, and Jain 1994).

The software provides two modes for calibrating the model: (1) by analogy and subsequent refinement (i.e., visual tracking), and (2) by fitting the Bass model to past data via nonlinear least squares (Srinivasan and Mason 1986). The forecasting component of GBass is set up for visual tracking: you can watch how changes in model parameters affect forecasts.

On the **Model** menu, select **Bass Model** (gbass.xls) to see the **Introduction** screen.

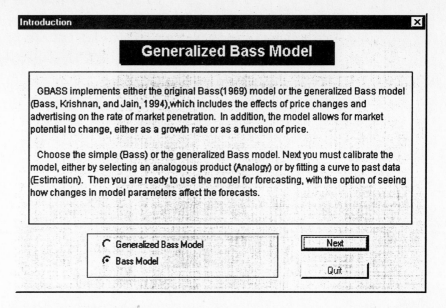

First select either the **Generalized Bass Model** or the **Bass Model** and click **Next**. The generalized Bass model includes two decision variables, pricing and advertising, which are assumed to determine the total number of customers. The Bass model sets up the original model without decision variables and assumes a constant number of customers.

Because the generalized Bass model includes the Bass model, we will describe its use. Both versions have the same setup.

Model calibration by analogy

The model includes a database that contains actual data points, estimated p and q coefficients, and estimates of market potential for various data sets to which the Bass model has been applied. The data come from several product categories.

You need to identify an analogous product or technology that has market characteristics similar to those of the product you want to analyze. When there are no past data for the product of interest, calibrating the model by analogy can be useful. This can also be useful when you don't have enough data to feel confident about estimating numerical parameters for the model.

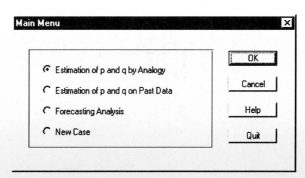

To explore the sales patterns of analogous products, select **Estimation of p and q by Analogy** and click **OK**.

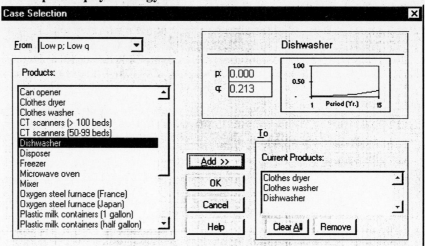

First select a category. All cases have been divided into four categories: (low p, low q), (high p, low q), etc. For example, a high p coefficient indicates a high coefficient of external influence, e.g., advertising was a significant driver for the market penetration of the product. A high q coefficient value indicates a high coefficient of internal influence, e.g., word of mouth was a significant driver for the market penetration of the product. When you click a product in the **Products** list, you will see a preview of its curve and its coefficients.

Now choose a product and click **Add>>** to add a product to the group of potential reference cases in the **Current Products** area. (Add no more than three products, since at most three curves can be graphed at a time.)

After you choose your cases and click **OK**, the program will chart the actual data points and the estimated diffusion curves for them.

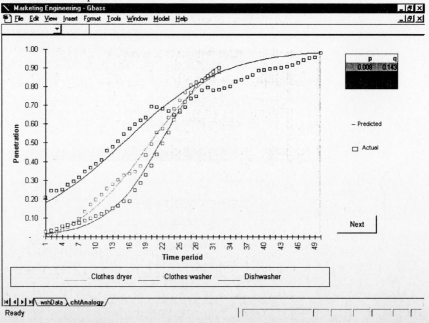

To simplify comparisons we have normalized the available cases to a maximum market penetration equal to 1.

Click **Next** to get to the next box. Indicate the product that you think offers the best analogy and that you want to keep for further reference.

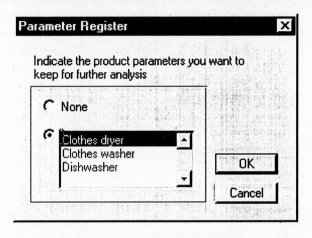

Click **OK** to get to the **Main Menu**.

Model calibration by estimation

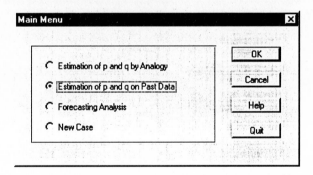

To estimate the model parameters numerically (using Solver), choose **Estimation of q and p on Past Data** and click **OK**. Enter the number of past periods for which you have data. Click **OK**.

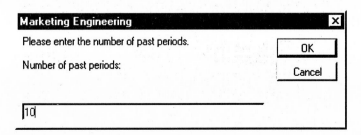

NOTE: *Once you have specified this number you will not be able to change it for subsequent estimations for this product. To make estimates for a different number of periods you must go to the **Main Menu** and select **New Case***.

Next, enter data for **Cumulative Sales Before Period 1, Market Growth Rate**, **Market Potential at Start** (your estimate of the total market size at the starting period), and **Market Potential Price Elasticity**.

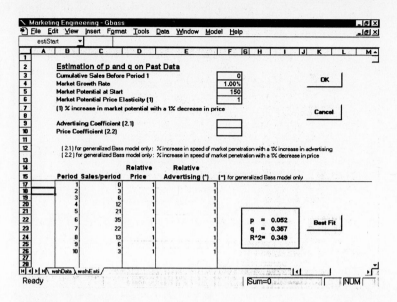

NOTE: *Period 0 serves as an anchor for the display of the curves. Sales in period 0 are always fixed to zero.*

If you chose the **Bass Model,** you don't need to provide values for the advertising or price coefficients. If you chose the **Generalized Bass Model**, you must provide estimates for these coefficients, because historical data rarely have enough variability to permit estimation of these parameters using past data. The advertising and price coefficients can be roughly thought of as "market acceptance speed elasticities," indicating the speed with which the market adopts the new product:

- The advertising coefficient reflects the percent increase in speed of market acceptance with a one percent increase in advertising. (Typical values for the advertising coefficient range between 0.3 and 1.)
- The price coefficient reflects the percent increase in speed of market acceptance with a one percent decrease in price. (Typical values for the price coefficient range between 1 and 2.)

Now enter the data on sales in each period and, optionally, an index for price and advertising in each period.

Click **Best Fit** to start the calibration of the model. The program estimates only the coefficients for p and q. The market potential estimate is fixed at your best guess input.

Click **OK** to go back to the **Main Menu**.

Forecasting analysis

Select **Forecasting analysis** and click **OK**.
You will see the following box:

(*) : % increase in market potential with a 1% decrease in price

Enter values for the **Number of Forecast Periods**, the **Market Growth Rate**, and the **Market Potential Price Elasticity** (that is, the percent increase in market potential with a one percent decrease in price). Click **OK**.

Next specify the expected course of price evolution. For the generalized Bass model you must also specify the evolution of advertising

effort. The relative price and relative advertising values are indices with
respect to their values in period 0, the last period for which actual data
are available.

Click **OK** to get to the next screen.

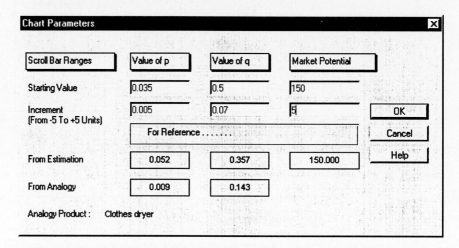

For charting and visual tracking, specify the starting values and increments for the coefficients p and q, and for the market potential. If
available, the program displays values from both the best-fit estimates
(estimation of p and q on past data) and the reference case (selection of p
and q by analogy).

NOTE: *The parameters can be varied by up to five increments on either
side of the* **Starting Value**.

Click **OK** to see the estimated sales curves.

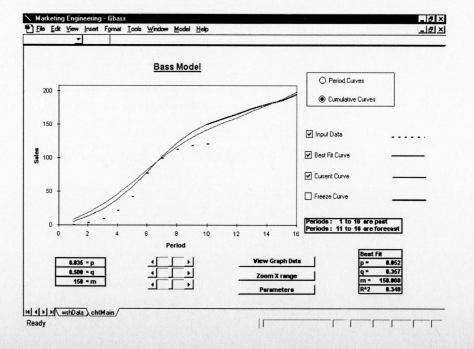

You can view the sales curves either period by period (**Period Curves**) or cumulatively (**Cumulative Curves**). Check the box to the left of **Current Curve** to see the forecasted sales pattern for the values of p, q, and n shown in the left bottom part of the screen. By using the scroll bars under **Period** you can adjust the parameters for the **Current Curve** and observe how changes in the parameter values affect the shape of the graph.

Once you think you have a reasonably good match between your **Input Data** (if available) and the **Current Curve**, you can freeze this curve as a benchmark. All the parameter values for **Freeze Curve** are displayed in the area in the lower right corner. Compare them to the parameter values for the **Best Fit Curve** if you checked that option. You can continue to change the shape of the **Current Curve**, and the **Freeze Curve** will remain fixed.

Clicking the **View Graph Data** button brings up a worksheet listing the raw data. You can only view and not change the data in this data sheet.

Clicking **Zoom X Range** allows you to limit the number of periods for which the data are plotted.

Clicking the **Parameters** button brings back the display **Chart Parameters**. You can enter new values for the starting points of the coefficients and increments.

If you want to try another case or another analogy, modify your data points, or save the current case, you need to bring up the **Main Menu**. To do so, go to the **Model** menu and choose **Main Menu**.

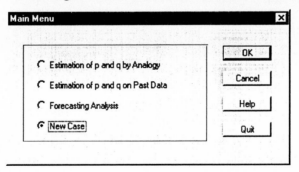

If you want to analyze another product, select **New Case** from the **Model Menu**. Decide whether you want to **Save** or **Discard** the current scenario.

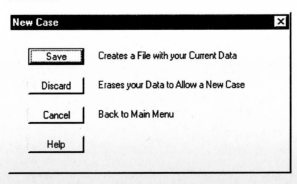

References

Bass, Frank M; Krishnan, Trichy V.; and Jain, Dipak 1994, "Why the Bass Model Fits Without Decision Variables," *Marketing Science,* Vol. 13, No. 3 (Summer), pp. 203-223.

Bass, Frank M. 1969, "A New Product Growth Model for Consumer Durables," *Management Science*, Vol. 15, No. 4 (January), pp. 215-227.

Srinivasan, V. and Mason, Charlotte H. 1986, "Nonlinear Least Squares Estimation of New Product Diffusion Models," *Marketing Science*, Vol. 5, No. 2 (Spring), pp. 169-178.

ZENITH HIGH DEFINITION TELEVISION (HDTV) CASE*

On August 1, 1990, Jerry Pearlman, CEO of Zenith Electronics Corporation, met with Bruce Huber, VP of marketing, to discuss the market potential for a new technology called high definition TV (HDTV). At the end of the meeting, Mr. Pearlman asked Mr. Huber to develop, within a month, a preliminary forecast of demand for HDTV sets for a 15-year period starting in 1992. Although they both realized that any forecasts they came up with would just be best guesses they still felt that forecasts would be useful in deciding whether and how the company should respond to this emerging technology. Many strategic decisions would depend on these forecasts, including the level and nature of the R&D and marketing research activities the company would undertake, the strategic alliances it would pursue to get a running start in the marketplace, and the extent of its participation in industrywide lobbying efforts with the FCC (Federal Communications Commission) and the US Congress.

HDTV background

As compared to conventional TV sets, HDTV sets produce better quality pictures with higher resolution and superior sound (CD-like). They also have wider screens. According to the Electronic Industries Association, high definition in TV can be measured by the resolution of the picture, that is, the number of horizontal and vertical lines scanned on the TV screen.

To promote the growth of HDTV several stakeholders would have to adopt a common set of standards:

- Technical specifications for the core functions and manufacture of HDTV sets
- Production standards to enable TV and movie studios to develop content to take advantage of the superior display features of HDTV
- Broadcast and transmission standards regulated by the FCC to ensure high quality transmission within the available frequency spectrum

The Japanese government and industry adopted an HDTV standard in 1984 that had 1125 lines per frame, while the US NTSC (National Television Standards Committee) standard is 525 lines per frame. In addition the US NTSC standard has a 4:3 (or 16:12) aspect ratio (ratio of frame width to height) but the committee is considering a wide-screen aspect ratio of 16:9 for HDTV. Movies made after 1950 typically used

---

* This is based on Harvard Business School case 5-591-025 and is used here with the permission of HBS Publishing Division.

wide-screen formats although not always with a 16:9 aspect ratio, while TV programs and most movies made before 1950 typically used a 16:12 aspect ratio.

The Japanese standard relied on traditional analog signals for broadcasts, but the transmission was only over satellite channels. Unless consumers had both an HDTV and a way to receive satellite signals, they would not be able to receive these programs.

In 1990, US industry and government were still working together on setting standards. They had to resolve several thorny issues:

Compatibility with existing TVs: The FCC wanted to ensure that whatever transmission standard the industry adopted for HDTV it would not make existing TV sets obsolete. Even with compatibility ensured, an HDTV program would leave the top and bottom of the screen empty when displayed on a standard TV set (Exhibit 1a). On the other hand, when receiving a standard-broadcast TV program, an HDTV would display a squarish picture in the middle of a wide rectangle (Exhibit 1b).

Digital versus analog standard: Several US firms including Zenith were pushing for adoption of digital standards instead of the analog standard the Japanese had adopted. Under a digital standard all images would be converted to the 0/1 language of computers and compressed before being transmitted by cable, satellite, or over the air. The TV receiver would convert the digital streams back into images.

Although a digital standard seemed to be better aligned with the expected convergence of computer and telecommunication technologies, industry members had several concerns. Analog signals typically degenerate gracefully under interference, i.e., a small loss of signal quality results in only a small loss of picture quality. Digital signals however tend to degrade substantially with a small impairment to the signal quality. This may not be a major problem for cable-based transmission. Also people have had a lot of experience with analog transmission. A digital transmission standard could require experimentation and testing over several years before adoption.

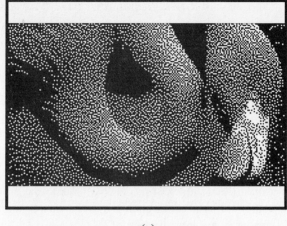

(a)

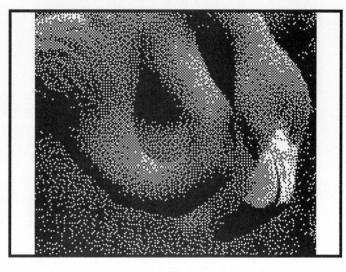

(b)

EXHIBIT 1
(a) HDTV broadcast as it appears on standard TV, and
(b) standard NTSC broadcast as it will appear on HDTV.

Regardless of whether the industry adopts a digital or analog transmission standard, content providers, such as TV and movie studios would have to invest in costly equipment to produce images with higher resolution. For example, studios would either need high-definition digital cameras for shooting or equipment to convert images from a high-resolution format, such as 35mm film. A studio-quality camera would cost around $300,000 to $400,000. Production staff at TV studios would also have to adapt to the new wide-screen-aspect ratio. They would have to learn new techniques for composing scenes, editing frames, and so forth. At the same time, broadcasters (e.g., TV stations and cable TV companies) would have to invest heavily in such equipment as transmitters and towers to broadcast HDTV signals.

Zenith HDTV efforts to date

In 1990, Zenith was working to develop advanced flat-screen picture tubes that could display images in the HDTV format. The development efforts looked promising, so Zenith anticipated marketing 20" and wider screens by 1992. In addition Zenith and its partner, AT&T, had made significant advances in developing a "spectrum compatible" HDTV transmission system that would offer HDTV pictures in the same channel space as existing NTSC standards. (Because of the scarcity of channel bandwidth such a system was considered to be a necessary element in the introduction of HDTV.)

The TV market

Zenith had conducted a number of studies of consumer behavior, which led to the following general conclusions:

- Consumers looked for value for their money and stayed within their budgets. Most consumers were satisfied with their existing TVs.
- Product quality was the most important criterion for evaluating brands. Consumers generally preferred large screens to small screens and considered such product features as stereo, remote control, and style to be important as well.
- Consumers tended to shy away from the lowest priced brands because they were suspicious of poor quality.

Bruce Huber had access to several additional sources of data acquired by Zenith's marketing research department. In particular he thought the data shown in Exhibits 2 to 7 might be useful in forecasting the sales of HDTV sets.

	Size	% units	Average retail price
Small	<19"	42%	$290
Medium	20-25"	40%	$610
Large	27+"	15%	$1,050

EXHIBIT 2
Breakdown of the TV set size distribution in 1989 and the corresponding average prices.

	TV households	Multi-set	Color TV	Cable	VCR	Remote control
1950	10%	–	–	–	–	–
1955	67	4%	–	–	–	–
1960	87	12	–	–	–	–
1965	94	22	7%	–	–	–
1970	96	35	41	7%	–	–
1975	97	43	74	12	–	–
1980	98	50	83	20	–	–
1985	98	57	91	43	14%	29%
1989	98	63	97	53	60	72
1990	98	65	98	56	66	77

Note: Nielsen estimated U.S. TV households = 92.1 million on Jan. 1, 1990.

EXHIBIT 3
Data on the market's time pattern for adoption of past TV-related technologies. *Source*: *The American Enterprise*, 1990, p. 97.

Year	Total units	Total $	Average $/unit	Total $ in 1989 $*	Avg. $/unit in 1989 $*
1971	11,197	$2,551,997	$228	$7,831,740	$698
1975	11,606	2,684,121	231	6,184,102	533
1980	18,143	4,798,239	264	7,220,650	398
1985	20,829	5,871,854	282	6,766,820	325
1989	24,669	6,899,762	280	6,899,761	280

*Adjusted for the Consumer Price Index

EXHIBIT 4
Summary of factory shipments of TVs in the U.S. since 1971. *Source*: EIA Electronic Fact Books 1981-1989.

Buyer type

Performance or feature	36%
Experience	34%
Price	30%

Note: Performance or feature-oriented buyers consider primarily the performance and the features of the set when making a TV purchase;

Experience-oriented buyers want technology they can trust, i.e., technology that is stable and has been widely used, before they adopt;

Price-oriented buyers base their purchases primarily on the price of the product.

EXHIBIT 5
Summary of the results of a market segmentation study of TV buyers conducted by Zenith.

	1989	1990	1991	1992	1993	1994
Color TV forecast (Econometric model)	22.0	22.2	23.4	24.9	25.7	25.9
—Units—						
First purchase	2.1	1.8	1.6	1.6	1.5	1.5
Replacement	7.7	8.3	8.9	9.6	10.3	11.0
Additional	11.6	11.5	12.3	13.0	13.2	12.7
Institutional	0.6	0.6	0.6	0.7	0.7	0.7

EXHIBIT 6
Zenith's forecast sales of color TVs by purchase occasion (millions of units).

	1992	1993	1994	1995	1996	1997	1998	1999	2000
Industry total (millions of units)	21.4	21.9	22.4	22.9	23.5	24.1	24.7	25.2	25.9
25" and larger (millions of units)	6.0	6.1	6.2	6.4	6.8	7.2	7.5	8.0	8.5
Zenith retail price for HDTV									
26"/31"	$2500	$2000	$1700	$1500	$1400	$1350	$1300	$1300	$1300
22"/27"				1100	1000	900	900	900	
Zenith retail price with conventional tube									
26"/31"	$3000	$2500	$2100	$1900	$1700	$1550	$1550	$1550	$1500
22"/27"				1200	1100	1000	1000	1000	

EXHIBIT 7
Zenith's forecasts of U.S. sales of large screen TVs, which have price points that are likely to be similar to those of the HDTV.

Forecasts of HDTV sales

A few months earlier, the Electronic Industries Association (EIA) had forecast that HDTV would penetrate 25 percent of US households by the year 2000. Jerry Pearlman was not that optimistic but still predicted that HDTV would garner about 10 percent of the TV industry sales by 1999.

Some industry observers believed that both of these forecasts were optimistic because picture quality alone won't sell HDTV sets without significant levels of HDTV programming and broadcasting. They believed that the projected levels of penetration would occur only if (1) the FCC settled on a transmission standard immediately, a highly unlikely prospect, and if (2) broadcasters invested substantial amounts of money in new equipment, which is unlikely before studios produce the content for HDTV broadcasting. There are about 1500 TV stations in the country, each of which would have to incur equipment costs of between $2 and 3 million to upgrade to digital transmission. These observers thought that neither of these scenarios was likely to occur for several years and that by the year 2000, sales would perhaps reach "a few hundred thousand units." Until then, HDTV would be used mostly for viewing closed-circuit TV programs, such as training films (e.g., surgery demonstrations), or for home-viewing of rented or owned movies on high-end entertainment systems.

With this preliminary research behind him, Bruce Huber was ready to tackle "the HDTV forecasting problem." He had recently acquired software called GBass for forecasting new-product sales. He wondered whether this software would be of any help in this forecasting task.

EXERCISES

1. Summarize and justify alternative scenarios (i.e., consistent sets of assumptions) ranging from pessimistic to optimistic with regard to market performance of HDTV.

2. Develop forecasts of HDTV penetration in the US market from 1992 through 2006 for each scenario you develop. Justify and explain your forecasts.